CW00601508

Finance and Profitability

THOROGOOD

THE PUBLISHING
BUSINESS OF THE
HAWKSMERE GROUP

Published by Thorogood Limited
12-18 Grosvenor Gardens
London SW1W 0DH.

Thorogood Limited is part of the
Hawksmere Group of Companies.

A CIP catalogue record for this Pocketbook is available
from the British Library.

ISBN 1 85418 064 9

Printed in Great Britain by Ashford Colour Press.

Designed and typeset by Paul Wallis at Thorogood.

Front cover: © Bridgeman Art Library
– *Tax Collecting* by Pieter Brueghel.

Business Action Pocketbooks

Business Information Pocketbooks are concise but comprehensive reference books designed to fit in your pocket or briefcase to be a ready source of business information. Each *Pocketbook* gives an introductory overview of a single topic and is followed by around 20 sections describing a particular aspect of that topic in more detail.

Pocketbooks will be of use to anyone involved in business. For owner managers and for managers in bigger businesses they will provide an introduction to the topic; for people already familiar with the topic they provide a ready reminder of key requirements. Each section concludes with a checklist of useful tips.

This book is based on *Business Information Factsheets* researched and written by enterprise and economic development agency, Project North East. Section contributors include Linda Jameson, Andrew Maville and Bill Waugh all of whom work at PNE. The series has been edited by David Irwin.

The information is checked by an independent expert to ensure, as far as possible, that it is accurate and up to date. However, neither the publishers nor the authors can accept any responsibility for any actions that you should take based on its contents. If you are in doubt about a proposed course of action, you should seek further professional advice.

Other titles in the 'Pocketbook' series

Business Action Pocketbooks are a series of concise but comprehensive reference books. Each one contains sections describing particular aspects of a topic in detail and checklists with useful tips.

Building Your Business

This *Pocketbook* provides practical information about growth, strategy and business planning. Effective leadership, problem solving, decision making and the formal aspects of running a business are also covered in this guide which will help to define your strategy and ensure that you achieve your stake in the future.

Managing and Employing People

Discover the key to successful people management by motivating, stimulating and rewarding your staff. Practical information and advice about recruiting staff, employee rights and obligations, effectively managing people and the legal aspects of employment are all covered in this *Pocketbook*.

Developing Yourself and Your Staff

Team building, personal development, managing meetings, stimulating staff and quality management are all covered in a clear and practical way for the busy manager in this *Pocketbook*. By developing your people through teamwork, training and empowerment you are developing your business – this book tells you how.

Sales and Marketing

This *Pocketbook* is an excellent reference tool focusing on the overall process of sales and marketing. It will help give you a direction and a set of goals along with practical tips and techniques for successful market research, segmentation and planning, promoting, selling and exporting. It will help you take those first important steps towards establishing a presence in your market.

Contents

Introduction

The importance of effective financial control

There are two over-riding requirements for every business: it has to make a profit and it has to generate cash. Without profit, you have nothing to reward the investors and are unable to reinvest in the business. Without cash, you are unable to pay the bills, and quickly become insolvent.

Whatever your business does, therefore, you need to have at least some form of plan and, crucially, you need financial forecasts. The forecasts will show whether you will make a profit and how much; they will show when you will generate cash, and when, perhaps, you need to borrow cash to cover short term requirements.

You can then monitor performance against that plan and, if required, take corrective action to ensure that the business remains profitable. Effective financial control can be achieved by monitoring a relatively small number of figures and identifying variations that require attention.

You will find retaining effective financial control far easier if you have an understanding of how to read the key financial statements – the profit and loss account, the balance sheet and the cash flow statement – and if you are able to calculate and use a small number of simple ratios.

Success and prosperity

If you are managing a department or division in a business or running your own business or managing a charitable organisation you will know how much courage, commitment and hard work is required to succeed and prosper. Success and prosperity requires successful marketing, successful financial control and success in managing and motivating your staff. Many people move into management because they are good 'at what they do', but they are not necessarily equipped at the outset to do everything well that managers have to do. In small organisations, in particular, there is an expectation that managers can do everything. In small businesses such tasks usually fall to the proprietor. For many managers, and for many entrepreneurs, exercising effective financial control is, at best, seen as a mystery and, at worst, not even considered. Yet monitoring a small number of important figures can ensure that you retain complete and effective financial control. This should ensure that the business stays profitable; it will certainly ensure that you are able to live within agreed borrowing facilities and that you are in a position to take corrective action before it is too late.

In a world of constant change and uncertainty some of this may be beyond your control, such as interest rates or the latest consumer fad. So managers and entrepreneurs have to concentrate their efforts on their strategy and on their marketing. All businesses experience problems. Many problems, however, need not arise if care is taken to ensure that you understand what is happening at all times. Look at how many businesses, apparently successful, have suddenly failed. Wildly exceeding your sales forecast can cause cash flow problems as severe as failing to reach the forecast. Those businesses which have an effective system of financial control will have more time available to worry about their marketing and more information to assist in developing their strategy.

Good financial results will not arise by happy accident. They will arrive by realistic planning and tight control over expenses. Remember that profit is the comparatively small difference between two large numbers – sales and costs. A relatively small change in either costs or sales can, therefore, have a disproportionate effect on profit.

You need, therefore, to watch very carefully your costs, prices and margins at all times since small changes in any can lead to substantial changes in net profit. Control can then be exercised by comparing actual performance with budget.

The importance of making a profit

Every business has to be seen to make a profit. Without a profit you cannot reward the investors for their stake in the business (including yourself if you are the sole investor), nor will you have enough money for reinvestment to make the business grow. And that profit has to come after paying all the staff as well as all the other expenses. To do that you need a product or service which is marketable and which you can persuade customers to buy at a price which exceeds the costs. For most businesses, prices tend to be market based so costs must be controlled to keep sufficiently below the price in order to make a profit.

Large companies generally aim to maximise their profits over the long term. This increases shareholder value and gives the investors a regular dividend. Private companies do not need to worry about profit maximisation if they choose not to. They are not vulnerable to takeovers and the shareholders may have other objectives. Working shareholders, sole proprietors or partners may agree, for example, to forego some of the potential profit because they prefer to work less hard. One of the great benefits of working for oneself is the opportunity to do work that is fun and rewarding. Of course, there will be tasks, as with any job, that may seem tedious and time-consuming, but overall I believe that owner managers should be seeking a balance between fun and reward. However, if they do not aim for a realistic profit, there is always the danger that they will make a loss and businesses which continually lose money quickly cease to trade.

If you have invested money in the business, is the reward greater than the opportunity cost? If you cannot do at least this well, you might decide that you would be better off working for someone else and reinvesting your money elsewhere. Similarly, if you need to borrow money from the bank, you need to ensure that you are generating a return that is considerably greater than the interest that you have to pay the bank, otherwise you end up working for the bank instead of yourself. Many people do not think carefully enough about the cost of borrowing money, only looking at the size of the monthly repayments. But cost is an important consideration, particularly if you are seeking a large sum of money, say, to buy equipment.

The importance of cash

Generating cash is at least as important as making a profit. In the early stages of a business it might even be more important. You need cash to pay your creditors – failing to pay your debts as they fall due means that the business is insolvent and is an offence. You will want to ensure, therefore, that you have enough current assets to cover your current liabilities. And you may need to look at ways of turning current assets into cash more quickly than simply waiting for your debtors to pay. This is where factoring or invoice discounting become important. Alternatively, you may need to negotiate a larger overdraft to provide the required level of working capital.

You need to have an idea, in advance, of how much cash will be required. Without a forecast, this will be impossible.

There may also be occasions when you need to borrow large sums of money, perhaps for short periods. This will be far easier if your business is profitable and if you can demonstrate to potential lenders, such as the banks, that you are in control and know the exact financial position of the business.

It is not enough, however, for businesses simply to aim to make a profit and to generate cash. If they do, they are likely to hop from one opportunity to another. The most successful businesses are usually driven by a clear sense of purpose and by core values shared widely by the staff.

Strategic objectives

It is essential for any business to set both long term and short term objectives. What is your purpose? You need a clear idea of why you are in business. You need to have a clear vision of where you are going. What are your 'big hairy audacious goals? If you do not have a vision you will not know when you get there, nor will you be able to monitor your progress. Lastly, you need to have some idea of what you are actually going to do to achieve your vision, that is, strategic objectives and how you intend to implement them.

Successful businesses are ones that use planning to provide themselves with a frame-work rather than a straightjacket. They still need to ensure that they can be responsive and flexible when opportunities arise. Without an element of planning, however, it is not possible to monitor progress and, more importantly, to take corrective action when you diverge too far from the plan.

Many small businesses think of strategic or long term planning as something that is only undertaken by large businesses. Your task is to match effectively the business's competences (that is, its knowledge, expertise and experience) and resources with the opportunities created by the market place. In other words, businesses should be market driven. This requires at least some thinking about the business, its place in the market place and the wider environment, about strengths, weaknesses, opportunities and threats and about where you would like to be in, say, five years time.

Businesses should define a purpose and goals which should ideally reflect the business's customers as well as what the business does to meet the needs of those customers. The strategy must support the purpose, it must fit the environment in which the business works but will be constrained by the resources that are available or can be attracted. It must be action focused. In the words of Peter Drucker, strategy 'converts what you want to do into accomplishment'.

Remembering that the primary reason for being in business is to make a return on the investment of your time and money, you should set a number of financial and marketing objectives (though marketing objectives are normally translatable into financial ones). These might include, for example:

- Market share or increase in market share
- Growth, measured by level of sales or increase in sales
- Level of profit or increase in profit
- Profitability, perhaps measured by return on investment or return on equity
- Level of productivity or improvement in productivity.

What are the key activities for success?

There are four aspects of running a business which need particular care if the business is to be successful.

- First, the business has to be able to provide a product or service efficiently, of the right quality, at an acceptable cost and at the right time.
- Second, the product or service must be effectively marketed to the prospective customer. It is important to satisfy the needs of your customers. When asked what his business did, Charles Revson, replied: 'In the factory we make cosmetics; in the store we sell hope'. In other words,

businesses sell features, but people buy benefits . The customer must be prepared to pay more for the benefits that they derive than it costs you to provide the features. The difference between cost and price is your profit.

- Third, you need to exercise tight financial control. It is extremely easy for the costs to run away, to waste materials and to sell products or services too cheaply. At best, this will reduce profit; at worst, the business will make a loss and, eventually, go out of business.

- Finally, you need to be aware of the business's human resource needs. Once a business starts to employ people you will have to think about recruitment, induction, career development, training, motivation, etc. This all costs extra money, but should be regarded as an investment in exactly the same way as you might expect to invest in machinery. The business depends on the people employed, so treat them properly.

Running a business or a unit within a business means that you are continually faced with a series of events for which decisions have to be taken. The right decisions depend upon having the right information easily available. This is as true for information about the business's financial position as for every other aspect of running the business.

Book-keeping

The starting point for effective financial control is in ensuring that you keep your books of account up to date and accurate. Book-keeping is extremely simple. All it requires is to enter the details of all transactions promptly, together with regular reconciliations to ensure it is accurate. If you have a very small business, then sales and purchase ledgers and a cash book will provide you with everything you need. Larger businesses will require a 'double-entry' system or, more likely, will computerise their book-keeping. An understanding of the basic principles, however, will help in identifying the errors which inevitably appear.

The books, of course, only give you the data – you have to turn that data into useful information. You will want to compare your actual sales with your forecasts – a graph on the wall is particularly effective! But achieving your sales is only part of the equation. You also have to work hard to keep costs under control. One effective technique is variance analysis – looking at where there are differences between forecast and actuals. You may also want to define costs in terms of a percentage of sales income. If sales fall, you will need to push down the costs, and a simple variance analysis may not pick that up fast enough.

You will also want to use figures from the books to produce monthly management accounts – a simple operating statement and balance sheet will suffice. Look at the key ratios – gross profit margins, net profit margins, current ratio, collection days, payment days – how are you performing? You may want to compare your performance with your own performance historically and with other businesses in the same sector.

Sources of finance

There are just three sources of finance for a business:

- Equity – money introduced by the owner(s), for which they expect a share of the profit, either as drawings for a sole proprietorship or partnership, or as dividends for a company;

- Loan finance – money typically borrowed from a bank, on which interest is payable and for which collateral may be required, or borrowed from trade creditors by delaying for as long as possible the paying of bills; or,

- Retained earnings – money earned by the business after paying all of its expenses, in other words, profit.

The sources of finance, usually called liabilities by accountants, are used to pay for the assets of the business.

You will be particularly anxious to speed up payment for your goods or services, because the faster you are paid the less working capital you require from one of these sources. If you have difficulty getting paid quickly you may, for example, want to look at factoring or invoice discounting. Whilst these have a cost, they do improve cashflow.

The working capital cycle

Clearly, you cannot simply spend, spend, spend unless there is sufficient money coming into the business to cover the expenditure, or unless arrangements have been made for finance to cover that expenditure.

In the production process a business takes raw materials; it adds value by turning those materials into a saleable product; and then it sells and dispatches the product to a customer. At each stage it may have stocks of raw materials or of work in progress or of finished goods.

Working capital cycle

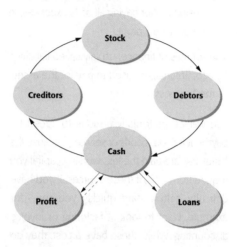

Following the cash is often more complicated than following the products! You may not pay immediately for what you buy. You will need to ensure that you have sufficient funds available to cover your stock, which includes raw materials, work in progress and finished goods. (Even if you are a service-based business you may well hold raw materials or have what is effectively work in progress.) Once you deliver those goods (or services) to your customer then you have sold them. You may not be paid for some time though. The eventual payment releases cash which can be used to pay your suppliers, to pay the fixed costs and to provide a profit. The money tied up in this way is known as working capital.

It is usually relatively straightforward to take decisions about capital expenditure. You can assess the need for a piece of equipment or a new vehicle; you can see what it will cost and know whether you have or can borrow the money. It becomes more difficult if you need more than one item but cannot afford everything, although there are techniques to help you choose.

It is considerably more difficult, however, to control working capital. Sometimes businesses discover that there is considerable demand for their product. They buy more stock, make more goods, sell more products – all apparently at a profit. They then discover that their customers do not pay soon enough whilst their suppliers are demanding payment. In other words, their working capital requirement has grown, but their actual growth in working capital has failed to keep pace with their growth in sales. This is known as over-trading.

A business is solvent if it has sufficient assets (cash, stock, debtors, fixed assets) to cover its liabilities (loans, creditors, etc). A business, however, also has to be able to meet its debts as they fall due. If it does not have sufficient cash, or sufficient assets which can quickly be turned into cash (often known as liquid assets), then it may be regarded as insolvent. Trading when knowingly insolvent is an offence, so care must be taken. Sole traders and partnerships have always had unlimited liability: that means that they are personally liable for all debts incurred by the business. Companies normally have limited liability: the shareholders will lose only their investment if the business fails. If it can be demonstrated, however, that the directors knew a company was trading whilst insolvent, then they can be held to be personally liable.

If sales are relatively stable, and if collection and payment periods are stable, there will be an equilibrium between current assets and current liabilities. If customers suddenly pay more slowly, or suppliers suddenly demand faster payment, or your sales start to increase, then the business will require an increase in working capital. Businesses can sometimes use their retained earnings to provide this additional working capital requirement but, if that is insufficient, the overdraft facility may need to be increased. Preparing cash flow forecasts, comparing performance against forecast, and regularly updating the forecast will assist in managing your working capital.

You will need to think carefully about all these needs and incorporate them, together with your sales forecast, into a budget. If you get your budgeting right, then you should have a fair idea of what your income and expenditure is likely to be during the year.

Budgeting

Once the financial objectives have been set, it is possible to prepare and agree a budget. A budget should restate the overall plan in figures. It differs from a forecast in the sense that the plan, and therefore the budget, sets minimum requirements, whereas a forecast is usually an expectation of what is most likely to happen. You might choose to budget for sales of £180,000 and you use this figure in calculating your likely expenditure, profit, etc. Based on your market research, however, you forecast sales of £200,000. You set a sales target of £220,000 in order to stretch your sales force. If all your costs are covered by the budgeted figure, then you will make a greater profit if you achieve the forecast and greater still if you achieve the target. Whilst this is an important distinction, in practice for most businesses the forecast and budget will be the same.

Appraising capital investments

One of the most important considerations in persuading others to back a project is the financial return that can be expected from the project. If the return is less than the cost of finance, or less than the opportunity cost if you already have funds available, then it is not worth proceeding. This is true whether you work for a large company and need to convince senior managers of the soundness of your proposal or you own a small business and must make a persuasive case to your bank or other providers of finance.

For projects involving substantial investments you will want to be able to assess the expected financial returns. You may want to compare returns on different possible projects. And different sources of funds, such as equity, debt and retained earnings, all have different costs.

There are a number of techniques which can be used to assess the possible returns and to achieve an appropriate balance between the various funding sources. Techniques include payback, return on capital employed, net present value and internal rate of return (IRR). IRR will also be of interest to you if you are seeking venture capital from an external investor – as they will normally look at their expected return in that way. If you understand what it means then you will be in a better position to negotiate.

Conclusion

Preparing financial forecasts, and using them to exercise tight financial control, is essential if you are to keep your business on track. It has been suggested that the most successful companies make greater use of equity and retained earnings and place far less reliance on loan finance. This enables them to think longer term, rather than having to work to meet the short term objectives of their funders. Whatever route you choose though, you ought to have a financial plan with objectives and targets, to monitor yourself against that plan and to take corrective action as necessary.

This *Pocketbook* will help you to understand how to use financial statements to manage your business and will suggest ways to manage your finances effectively.

Costing

part
one

1 Costing a product or service

This section covers the requirements for determining the costs of your business, identifying your break even point and setting a price for your product or service.

Different types of cost

It is helpful to divide up costs into different categories. Direct costs are those that can be directly attributed to the production of a particular product or service. Raw materials and subcontract labour are direct costs. Deducting the direct costs from the sales revenue for a particular product gives its 'contribution' towards overheads and profit. This is also known as the gross profit.

Variable costs vary in proportion to the level of production. These include direct costs. Some overhead costs, however, such as use of electricity, may also vary with total production even though they are difficult to allocate directly.

Fixed costs, on the other hand, do not vary in the short term and are not dependent on the level of production. These include rent, rates, insurance, managers' salaries, etc.

Indirect costs are the opposite of direct costs – those costs that cannot be directly attributed to a specific product. Fixed costs are always indirect; variable costs might be direct or indirect. In this section, the term 'direct costs' will be used to refer to costs directly attributable to the product or service being offered. The term 'overheads' will be used to cover all the other expenses of running the business.

If you are self-employed (as a sole trader or a partner) the money available to you is the profit, ie the sales revenue less all the costs. You will need to draw money out from the business on a regular basis. Remember that your drawings are simply an advance against profit. You are taxed on all the profit. For the purpose of calculating costs, it makes sense to treat your drawings and any income tax as overhead costs.

Manufacturing cost

If you are manufacturing, you can calculate the cost per item by:

$$\text{Item cost} =$$

$$\frac{\text{Business overheads}}{\text{Total items}} + \text{Direct cost of item}$$

COSTING A PRODUCT OR SERVICE

If you make more than one product, you need to split the business overheads between the different products, for example on the basis of the volume of each product.

Imagine that you make desks. You have estimated your total overheads for the year as £30,000 including depreciation, drawings and tax. You expect to make and sell 100 desks during the year. The cost of wood and other materials for each desk is £50. Using the equation:

$$\text{Item cost} = \frac{30,000}{100} + 50 = £350$$

You then need to add a profit margin, say 10 per cent, and VAT at 17.5% if you are registered for VAT. This gives a selling price of £452.

Service based businesses

If you provide a service, you will need to know how much to charge per hour, though you may estimate the total time required and offer your customers a fixed price when quoting. This can be expressed by:

$$\text{Hourly rate} = \frac{\text{Annual business overheads}}{\text{Annual productive hours}}$$

Remember that not all your working hours will be productive. Some time will be required for promoting your business, buying supplies, doing the books, etc. You will need some holidays and you should also allow for possible illness.

Imagine that you are a photographer. As above, your total overheads for the year are £30,000. After allowing for holidays, illness, etc you estimate that you will be able to sell 200 days of your time. You expect to average 7.5 hours per day.

Thus, your hourly rate $= \dfrac{30,000}{1,500} = \text{£}20/\text{hour}$

You need to add the direct costs (film, developing, printing, etc), profit margin and VAT. For a one day assignment you will charge time (£150) + direct costs (say £40) + profit (say 20%) + VAT (17.5%), giving a total price of £268.

Break-even analysis

Once you know your costs and estimated selling price, then you are in a position to calculate how many products, or hours of your time, you need to sell to break-even, ie to cover all your costs. Any further sales then provide you with a profit. The easiest way to do this is to draw a graph, showing your costs and income.

First show the overhead costs

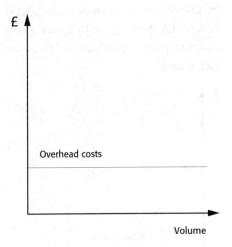

The direct costs can then be shown. These are added to the overheads to show the total cost for a given volume of output.

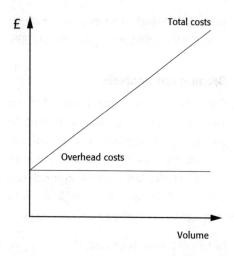

The sales income can then be plotted. This is shown overleaf on a graph by itself. It shows how much income will be generated for a given level of sales.

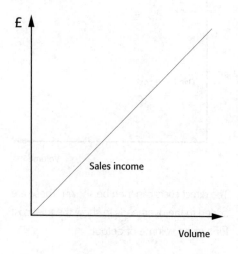

These can now be combined into a single break-even chart. The point where the sales income equals the total cost shows the break-even point. A higher price will give a break-even point after fewer sales. A lower price may attract more customers. The higher above break-even that a business can operate, the greater its margin of safety.

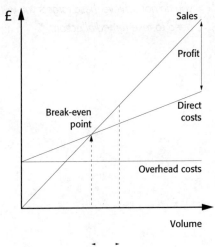

Margin of safety

- *Keep a close eye on your budgeted income and expenditure. If sales are not as high as required, recalculate your unit cost and sales price.*

- *Use your break-even sales volume to set monthly and annual sales figures. If you do not achieve these targets you will need to take remedial action.*

2 Budgeting

This section looks at the process of budgeting for the start up and growing business.

Introduction

The starting point for budgets and financial forecasts is the setting of strategic and operational objectives. A key set of operational objectives each year should cover sales targets. Normally, budgets are only set for the short-term. Most small businesses will find it sufficient to set budgets for the next financial year and little further. For start up businesses, clear and realistic budgeting is one of the first things potential funders will look for in a business plan.

A budget is not a forecast. Whilst it clearly has to be based on forecasts, it is your target. In setting sales targets, and a budget, you are committing yourself to perform to a certain standard. If budgeting and financial forecasting is going to be an effective tool for your business, you need to ensure that your accounting system is capable of monitoring your financial performance against the targets. You will then be able to monitor progress and take corrective action where necessary.

The sales budget

The sales budget is required to provide overall targets; you will need it to prepare other budgets. It should set out the number of units that you might be able to sell at a given price broken down by product, area, timing, etc.

Do your best, each time, to look at the total market and your likely share. Is the market expanding or contracting? Talk to your major customers about their likely purchases from you next year. Are you planning additional marketing? What will be its likely effect? Will you be putting up your prices? If so, how might that affect sales? Use all this information to predict as accurately as possible your sales forecast both by volume and value. If you sell more than one product, sales budgets should be prepared for each of them (don't forget to include any new products). If you sell in more than one area, then it may be helpful to have a sales budget for each of these. Ideally, you should aim to produce your sales budget on a monthly or quarterly basis.

The production budget

Once the sales budget has been determined, you should be able to prepare a production budget. This budgets for those costs which vary with the level of production: mostly just the direct costs. Don't forget to include subcontract and direct labour costs if appropriate to your business. The materials usage budget, subcontract budget and direct labour budgets should reflect the sales budget. This will assist in identifying surplus or shortfalls. If you use salespeople working on commission, their commission is usually shown as a direct (ie variable) cost (though their retainer, if they have one, would be a fixed cost). Discounts are usually shown in the budget as a direct cost (even though in reality a discount is simply income foregone).

If there are other variable costs, such as electric power consumption, these should be assessed to give a total production budget.

The materials purchase budget

If you have a manufacturing business, the next step after the sales budget is to look at the raw materials holding and ordering requirements.

Your purchasing policy should be reviewed regularly to ensure that you are obtaining value for money from suppliers and are paying the lowest possible price consistent with the quality desired. If there are likely to be delays in receiving raw materials after ordering them, you will need to hold sufficient stocks to cover production for the typical period of delay. This ties up working capital, however, so your target should be to keep raw materials to a minimum. You may be able to identify possible discounts or rebates which can also be built into the materials budget.

Once raw materials have been issued to production they become 'work in progress'. Work in progress valued at least at the cost of the raw materials that are now in production is often shown on the balance sheet (see section eight), though arguably it has no value until there is a product capable of being sold. If the manufacturing process is a long one, then the value added at each stage (labour, resources, etc) also has to be financed until the product is sold so this increases the working capital requirement.

When preparing the production budget, remember to monitor the number of machine hours available, the number of labour hours available, etc. If you exceed your capacity you may have problems. On the other hand, you do not want expensive machinery lying idle. So you should also look at your utilisation rates – if they are too low, can you raise them, perhaps by increasing sales or introducing new products?

The overheads budget

Once the production budget has been prepared, the other costs need to be calculated. If you are in manufacturing, it is likely that these will represent a relatively small proportion of the total costs. On the other hand, if you are running a service sector business, it is likely that overheads will represent a very high proportion, or indeed, all of the cost. If you have decided to use ratios which assess costs as a proportion of sales, then it makes sense to build up your overheads budget using the same cost groupings. Don't forget to include overhead costs which appear 'below the line' such as interest or drawings.

You may, if you choose, aim to allocate the overheads to each product or you may prefer to retain overheads as a single budget. You will, however, have to ensure that the price for each product makes a reasonable contribution to the overheads.

The production cost budget

You are now in a position to pull together the production budget and the overheads budget into a single production cost budget. If you have more than one product or service, then you will have a production budget for each. You will also have variable overheads to add for each product. There is no need to split fixed overheads across products at this point, since you are trying to determine the total costs. On the other hand, if some of the costs have been collected on a product or a departmental basis, then it probably makes sense to keep them separate, even at this stage, provided they are all included.

The capital expenditure budget

If you expect to spend large sums on capital equipment, then you need to set a budget and determine likely timing for those purchases. This is essential information if you are to prepare an accurate forecast, particularly where you may have to take out a loan to finance the purchase and will have to meet a repayment schedule which includes interest.

If you decide to lease equipment, make sure that you read all the small print. While the selling is carried out by your supplier, the leasing is done by a finance company. Usually the conditions are more favourable for them than for you. On the other hand, the lessor usually has a responsibility to ensure the equipment keeps working even if the supplier can no longer support you.

Presenting your results

Once the budgets have been prepared, you can use the data accumulated to prepare the cash flow forecast. This sets out on a month by month basis all cash inflows and outflows from the business, for the following 12 months.

USEFUL TIPS

● *Prepare budgets as early in the year as possible; this allows you plenty of time to assess potential financial requirements.*

● *Budgets are among the key areas of the business plan for potential funders' requirements.*

3 Keeping your costs down

This section looks at ways of increasing profitability through the control and minimising of costs.

Introduction

The basis of any business is that income should exceed expenses. Profitability can be improved by increasing sales, but it can also be enhanced through the reduction of costs. A business which keeps its costs under control will be able to release more resources for growth in the good times and will be in a better position to survive in recession.

Managing your costs

Cost control is only possible in a well organised, well managed business.

i)   To control costs you first need to know about them. Each cost should be identified clearly and you should keep a record of bills, etc.

ii) Costs need to be reviewed on a regular basis. This will depend upon when you normally do your accounts. It's not enough to calculate whether you are in profit or loss, you also need to be aware of what your normal costs are so that you can spot anomalies and take corrective action.

iii) Some costs will be more important than others to control. You will need to know which your critical costs are and concentrate upon reducing them.

iv) Cost control is the responsibility of everyone working in the business. Each employee has countless opportunities to affect costs throughout each day. If they are not happy at work, they are in a position to do a lot of damage. If they are motivated and feel part of the business they will work economically without supervision. Solving such problems is a test of good management; one approach is to involve employees in coming up with ideas to reduce costs.

v) Many people assume that because the volume of expenditure is so much larger than they are used to in home life, any savings they might make are insignificant. Informing staff about the impact of significant costs on profitability can help change such attitudes.

Direct cost control measures

Cost benefit analysis

The awareness of cost should be part of the planning process. In meetings, planning sessions or in personal planning the overall impact of any decision should be understood in terms of business profitability, ie the benefits of a particular course of action should be set against the cost. Such errors are frequently manifest in a failure to cost the time of staff. For example, a person may be assigned to carry out a piece of research which could be done more quickly by a consultant or bought off the shelf. The work may in fact have an insignificant impact on profitability, so was it worth doing at all? In such cases managers need to be quite pragmatic and ruthless.

Value analysis

Value analysis takes each part of a product, service or system and subjects it to detailed examination to see if there is any way in which its costs could be reduced without affecting quality. VA is usually done in a group. Each aspect of the product is challenged with questions such as: is it necessary, can it be made with cheaper materials, can it be bought cheaper than it costs to make, can it be made quicker, can it be simplified to reduce potential faults, can you use less material, can you reduce wastage, etc? VA is also a good way to involve employees and increase general awareness of cost control. You may wish to introduce environmental considerations – how does the production of components affect the environment, can they be recycled? Economising on your use of raw materials is one of the most effective cost saving measures you can take.

Purchasing methods

It goes without saying that significant savings may be derived from good purchasing practice. Generally speaking you should:

a) Look for discounts for buying in bulk

b) Be prepared to haggle; and

c) Review the cost of supplies and suppliers on a regular basis.

No bill or invoice the business receives should be taken for granted. You could persuade your landlord to reduce your rent if you think it is unfair. If you feel your rates are too high you can appeal to have your rateable value reduced (contact your local Inland Revenue Valuation Office for the relevant forms).

Stock control

Stock control is another area for savings. Accurate control will reduce storage and working capital costs. Effective security should reduce the cost of stock lost through theft.

Common centres for cost control

Staff

Staff costs often contain the greatest scope for savings. Can you employ fewer people to do the same thing? Are they motivated and monitored appropriately to ensure they deliver value for money? Is their remuneration appropriate – too much is costly, too little may lead to a high staff turnover (which is costly too) and may impair performance. Professional management techniques will increase the value you get from your staff.

Energy

Staff should be encouraged to use energy responsibly in the same way as they do at home. Most people today care about the environment, and this can motivate them to save energy. Bills should be checked for any anomalies. It is worth having your meters double checked, especially if you use a lot of energy. Ensure that your thermostats are set correctly. Do not underestimate the impact of proper insulation measures which can produce long term savings. You may be eligible for grants to insulate your property. The Department of Energy say that British businesses use 20% more energy than they need; their Energy Efficiency Office provides free advice and information.

Telephone

It is reasonable for staff to make necessary private calls from work, but some people do take advantage. Rules for personal calls should be made clear and action taken to discipline offenders. It is now possible to get itemised bills for each extension which should make such liberties more difficult. Staff should also be trained in the efficient use of the telephone to reduce the length of calls.

Copying

Photocopies and lasercopies are easy to use and the expense can soon get out of control if they are not kept an eye on. All copies should be logged, allocated to a cost centre, and the initials of the person taking the copy recorded. Staff should be charged for personal copies, and discouraged from making unnecessary copies. Someone should be made responsible for monitoring copying and usage should be reviewed regularly.

Stationery

Many people take home office stationery for their own use as a matter of course. Keep the store cupboard locked, and make someone responsible for issuing materials.

Expenses

Reduce misuse of expenses by drawing up clear guidelines so that everyone is clear upon what is and is not acceptable. Expense claims should be cleared by a responsible person before being paid. Expenses for individuals should be reviewed periodically and anomalies investigated.

Recycling

Recycling is good for the environment, and can save you money. All waste should be examined for potential recycling or resale to recycling companies. For example, there are companies who will buy industrial plastic waste for recycling. Scrap paper can be recycled as stapled writing pads. You can send off your used laserprinter cartridges to be refilled at a discount price.

- *Beware of false economies. If you provide an inappropriate level of service you could lose sales. If working conditions are too spartan, staff will be demoralised and will not perform.*

- *Confront your cost problems immediately. Don't put off dealing with your cost problems in the hope that they will go away. Take immediate action before the problem gets out of hand.*

- *Failure to plan ahead can be costly. Planning improves the efficiency of subsequent action, and reduces the chances of having to start again from scratch. The same applies to individuals. Staff should be aware of the value of their time and be trained to use time management techniques to improve their efficiency.*

- *Cost control depends upon efficient accounting practice. Use an accountant to help you establish suitable systems and advise on cost control. Accountants should be particularly helpful in advising on possible tax savings.*

4 **Depreciation**

This section explains the concept of depreciation and outlines two methods for calculating levels of depreciation.

Introduction

When calculating the price you will charge for your product or service you will need to determine all the costs of providing the product. Most costs, such as your time, rent, materials, etc are relatively straightforward to calculate, but how should you recover the cost of equipment which you expect to last more than one year? How should you allow for the fact that the equipment will eventually lose value (due to obsolescence, general wear and tear, or the passing of time) and will need to be replaced? The answer is through including a figure for 'depreciation' in the fixed costs.

Depreciation is an annual allowance for wear and tear of equipment. Since fixed assets generally have a life greater than one year, it would clearly be unreasonable to attempt to recover the entire cost from your customers in the year of acquisition. Instead, the cost of the wearing out is spread over the expected life of the asset.

Equipment, machinery, vehicles and industrial buildings (but not land) are depreciated.

To calculate the annual depreciation, you need to estimate the expected life of the asset and be able to estimate any residual or scrap value, although this is often simply regarded as zero. The aim of depreciation is to deduce a fair charge for the use of fixed assets, ensure that this is passed on to your customers, and to give a fair profit figure on your profit and loss account.

There are two main methods for calculating depreciation: straight line and reducing balance.

Straight line depreciation

Straight line depreciation writes off a percentage of the purchase price each year. For example, if a vehicle costing £12,000 has an expected life of four years and a scrap value of nil, then 25% of cost (ie £3,000) will be charged to the profit and loss account.

Imagine Yvonne has bought new equipment worth £30,000. She estimates that this will last seven years and have a scrap value of £2,000. The annual depreciation is, therefore £4,000. This figure is included as one of the fixed costs in the profit and loss account. The 'book-value' of the fixed assets, as shown on the balance sheet, is reduced by this amount each year.

Straight line depreciation

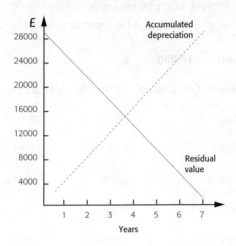

Reducing balance depreciation

Reducing balance depreciation is calculated as a percentage of the residual value of the equipment. This gives the highest level depreciation in the first year, reducing as the equipment ages. This gives a truer reflection of the real value of the equipment, as anyone who has bought a new car knows! Additionally, as the equipment ages it might be expected that costs for repairs will increase each year. If the total cost of depreciation and repairs remains about constant, then calculating the price to charge your customers remains quite simple.

Yvonne decides to use the reducing balance method, writing off her equipment over seven years. She charges 32% depreciation annually.

Cost	£30,000	£		£
Year 1	Depreciation	9,600	Balance	20,400
Year 2		6,528		13,872
Year 3		4,440		9,432
Year 4		3,018		6,414
Year 5		2,053		4,361
Year 6		1,396		2,965
Year 7		949		2,016

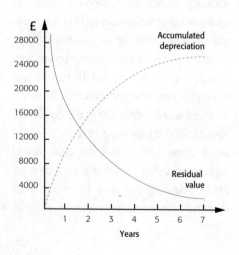

If you know how many years it will take to depreciate fully a piece of equipment, then you can calculate the rate, r, from this equation:

$$r = 100 - \left(\sqrt[n]{\frac{\text{residual value}}{\text{original cost}}} \times 100 \right)$$

where n = estimated life in years.

Tax consideration

Do not confuse depreciation with capital allowances for tax purposes. You may choose any level of depreciation that you think is appropriate. When you submit your accounts to the Inland Revenue, they remove depreciation completely from their calculation of your net profit. They then allow a capital allowance, generally of 25%, on a reducing balance basis. For industrial buildings they allow 4% pa. There is no allowance for commercial buildings.

If you expect equipment, eg computers, to last less than four years, then write them off faster. Remember, the more accurately you reflect depreciation in your budget the more accurately you will be able to cost your product or service.

Building up reserves

Depreciation is simply a 'book transfer'. It does not involve any transfer of money, nor does it build up reserves to replace equipment in the future. If possible, therefore, you should aim to put aside a sum at least equal to the annual depreciation (preferably higher to allow for inflation) to ensure that you have the cash available when equipment does need to be replaced.

USEFUL TIPS

- *When estimating the useful life of the asset, give due regard to anticipated changes in technology or market requirements.*

- *It is difficult to estimate the likely sale value at the end of the perceived useful life. It is advised that where the value is considered to be very small in relation to the cost, it should be treated as nil.*

Keeping accurate records

part
two

Keeping
accurate
records

part
two

5 Sales and purchase ledgers

This section outlines the requirements of maintaining a simple sales ledger and a simple purchases ledger.

Introduction

There are three key books of accounts necessary for adequate financial control. These are the cash book, the sales ledger and the purchase ledger. If you employ staff, then you will also require a wages book. All these records can be maintained in simple cash analysis books available from any office stationer. Computerised accounts packages are becoming more widespread and user friendly, but it is important that you understand the basic process of balancing a sales/purchases ledger.

The sales ledger

The sales ledger records all the sales for the month, the amount of cash received and shows what is due to the business at the end of the month. Every time an invoice is issued it should be recorded in the sales ledger. A copy of the invoice should be retained, showing:

a) The details of the work for which the invoice has been issued

b) A unique invoice number, and, if VAT registered

c) The VAT rate

d) The amount of VAT.

A typical format for a sales ledger is shown in Figure 1 (opposite). As can be seen, there is a column to enter the date when an invoice is paid. It is thus extremely easy to see which invoices are outstanding in order to chase them. This format will also satisfy the requirements for accounting for VAT.

Adding up the total invoices and the outstanding debtors at the end of each month will help in the preparation of management accounts.

The ledger is a continuing rolling forward record. Debtors who are still outstanding at the end of the month should be carried forward by recording the amount they owe at the bottom of the page. This amount will carry forward each month and unless you find yourself with 'bad debts' eventually the debtors figure will reduce to zero. Further columns can be added to differentiate between various types of sales (net amounts).

Sales ledger

Invoice date	Customer	Invoice no.	Net amount	VAT	Total	Date paid
1/9	PNE	9101	1000.00	175.00	1175.00	
4/9	TEC	9102	2000.00	350.00	2350.00	25/9
7/9	Bloggs	9103	500.00	87.50	587.50	26/9
12/9	PNE	9104	1000.00	175.00	1175.00	
Totals			4500.00	787.50	5287.50	
Outstanding debtors (end of September)					2350.00	

The purchase ledger

Many people are rather cavalier with purchase invoices (or bills), often tossing them in a desk drawer until the end of the month. Whilst this is simple, it is bad practice. You do not know how much you owe to your suppliers or even whether you still have all the bills – some are sure to get mislaid resulting in being unpaid, which therefore upsets suppliers.

The purchase ledger is used to record all purchase invoices and to show those which are still unpaid (and allow VAT to be accounted for). Though not entirely necessary, it may be helpful to use a format similar to the payments side of the cash book, though it excludes columns, such as wages, for which you do not receive bills. As with the sales ledger, the VAT figures can be quickly extracted when required (see opposite).

Whilst it is not essential to use purchase order numbers, it makes good sense. If you use a purchase ledger, you will be able to number the bills as they are received and record the number in the ledger so that you can easily retrieve the bill if a query arises later.

As with the sales ledger, every time a payment is made, it should be noted in the 'date paid' column. It is then very easy at the end of each month to note all those purchase invoices

Purchase ledger

Date received	Supplier	Ref no.	Total	VAT	Materials	Travel	Premises	Date paid
1/9	Northern Plumbing	991	117.50	17.50			100.00	
5/9	Premier Paper	992	235.00	35.00	200.00			
7/9	Alan's Garage	993	58.75	8.75		50.00		25/9
12/9	Rent	994	500.00				500.00	25/9
Totals			911.25	61.25	200.00	50.00	600.00	

Outstanding creditors
(end of September) 352.50

which are still outstanding and to make a note at the bottom of the page. This will help in the preparation of management accounts.

Remember that your financial information management system is only as good as the person running it. To ensure that you keep in control you should:

- *Record sales in the sales ledger as soon as the invoice is written.*

- *Record receipts in the sales ledger as soon as invoices are paid.*

- *Record purchases in the purchase ledger as soon as purchase invoices (ie bills) are received but, if there is likely to be a delay in receiving a bill, do it as soon as the order is placed.*

- *Record payments in the purchase ledger when you issue the cheque to pay the bills.*

- *Reconcile both ledgers every month.*

- *Chase all outstanding debtors every month.*

6 **The cash book**

This section outlines the requirements for maintaining a cash book summarising all financial transactions for your business.

Introduction

As noted in the previous section, there are three key books of accounts necessary for adequate financial control. These are the cash book (sometimes called the nominal ledger), the sales ledger and the purchase ledger. All these records can be maintained in simple cash analysis books though, as your business grows, you may wish to computerise all these.

The cash book

Look at the table overleaf which shows a typical cash book layout. An analysis cash book should be used which has a number of columns across the page. The number and headings of the columns will depend on the categories of receipts and payments which are likely to be incurred regularly.

There should be at least a 'sales' column and an 'other' column on the receipts page. The payments page may include columns, for example, for raw materials, travel, premises'

A typical cash book layout

Receipts

Date	Details	Ref no.	Bank	Sales ledger	Other
	c/forward		250.00		
24/9	TEC	9102	2350.00	2350.00	
25/9	BANK INT.	DD	200.00		200.00
26/9	Bloggs	9103	587.50	587.50	
TOTALS			3137.50	2937.50	200.00

Payments

Date	Details	Ref no.	Bank	VAT	Purchase ledger	Travel	Premises	Wages	Other
24/9	Petrol		23.50	3.50		20.00			
25/9	Alans Garage	993	58.75		58.75				
25/9	Rent	994	500.00		500.00				
27/9	Wages		1000.00					1000.00	
TOTALS			1582.25	3.50	558.75	20.00		1000.00	

Balance: 1555.25 (ie 3137.50 – 1582.25) • Carried down: 1805.25 (ie 1555.25 + 250 c/forward) costs, capital expenditure, staff wages, drawings, etc. It is conventional for receipts to be recorded on the left-hand page and payments on the right-hand page.

If the sales and purchases ledgers include VAT, then do not record VAT again in the cash book for the same transaction. Similarly, do not analyse receipts and payments individually in the cash book if they have already been analysed in the sales and purchases ledgers. These items should be analysed as 'Sales ledger receipts' and 'Purchases ledger payments' respectively.

Every time a cheque is received or issued, the total amount should be entered in the column headed 'Bank' on the relevant page and then analysed into the appropriate columns. This immediate analysis is to enable you to monitor the major and the most important items. Payments made by standing order or direct debit should also be recorded. Note the extra entries for wages and petrol which are not included in the purchase ledger.

At the end of the month all the columns should be totalled. The sum of the separate totals should equal the addition of the total (ie the bank) column. At the end of each month deduct the payments (£1,582.25) from the income (£3,137.50) to give the net cash flow for the month. Then add the figure carried forward from the previous month to give the carry down figure (£1,805.25). This is also the balance that should be in the bank. If the figure is negative, ie you have an overdraft – you should carry it forward on to the expenditure page.

Bank reconciliation

This is the process of comparing your cash book with your bank statement to make sure that they match. When you have allowed for uncleared cheques that have been paid to you and that you have paid out, you will know what the cash position of your business is.

The cash book should exactly represent every movement on the bank account. At the end of each month, you should reconcile the cash book with your bank statement. This is a means of ensuring that the cash book and statements do agree. Compare the bank with the cash book. If there are additional items, such as bank charges, interest, standing orders, etc, then these should be recorded in the cash book.

Any cheques issued or received close to the end of the month may not clear through the banking system in time to be included on your bank statement.

Reconcile the figures by taking the bank balance calculated from your records. Deduct uncleared receipts. Add uncleared payments. If the figure you get is not the same as on your bank statement, you have an error somewhere. Perhaps a payment or receipt has cleared sooner than expected.

Bank reconciliation	£
Bank balance (according to cash book)	1805.25
Less: uncleared receipts	– 587.50
Plus: uncleared payments	+ 1000.00
Calculated balance	= 2217.75
Bank statement balance	2217.75
Difference	0.00

It is important to monitor the timing of payments so that you do not go over the overdraft limit (if any) agreed with your bank. Even if your cash flow forecast shows a positive balance at the end of every month, there may be occasions during the month when this problem might arise.

● *Whenever you make a transaction, record it in your cash book. Otherwise, you will find it difficult to keep your records correct.*

● *Carry out a bank reconciliation every month. Not only will this help you keep track of your bank balance, it is far easier to find errors if you know that they cannot be more than one month old.*

● *Ask your bank to time the sending out of your bank statements for the end of each month, so that they coincide with the end of each of your accounting periods.*

Financial
statements

part
three

7 Cash flow forecast

Every business has to watch very carefully both its cash position and its profit. Forecasting your cash needs is essential and is best done with a cash flow forecast. This section reviews the steps required to prepare a forecast.

Introduction

A cash flow forecast sets out, usually on a month by month basis for the following 12 months, all receipts and all payments for a business. It is essential to know how much money a business will need, and the forecast provides a useful tool with which to analyse potential requirements, for example cash to buy in raw materials to meet a large order, etc.

For start-up businesses it is particularly useful to be able to determine exactly how much finance will be required to take the business through its early stages, and to pinpoint when the money will be needed. Indeed, the cash flow forecast is probably the key part of any business plan from the point of view of potential funders.

The forecast structure

As the example opposite shows, the typical forecast is split into three sections:

i)   Receipts – all money coming into your business, eg sales, loans, etc

ii) Payments – the money that you pay out

iii) Balances – the monthly balances and the cumulative balance.

The cash flow only shows cash in and out, so non-cash items such as depreciation (ie loss in value of assets through wear and tear or the passing of time) are ignored. In order to make the forecast you will probably need to prepare budgets for the year ahead, eg to assess how much you need to spend throughout the business.

A cash flow forecast

	July	August	Sept	Total
Sales by value	3,900	5,100	6,300	15,300
Receipts				
Cash	1,300	1,700	2,100	5,100
Debtors	1,200	2,500	3,000	6,700
VAT	437	735	892	2,064
Loans				
Total	2,937	4,935	5,992	13,864
Payments				
Trade creditors	1,000	1,300	1,700	4,000
Wages etc	1,000	1,000	1,000	3,000
Overheads	1,000	1,000	1,000	3,000
Equipment			3,000	3,000
Loan repayments	200	200	200	600
Overdraft interest		6	6	12
Drawings	1,000	1,000	1,000	3,000
VAT	350	403	997	1,750
VAT to C & E	500			500
Total	5,050	4,909	8,903	18,862
Balance	(2,113)	26	(2,911)	(4,998)
Opening balance	1,800	(313)	(287)	1,800
Closing balance	(313)	(287)	(3,197)	(3,198)

Receipts

Sales

This row shows sale by value, ie selling price multiplied by number of sales. You need to forecast your likely sales for the next year as accurately as possible. Don't just look at the sales you need to cover your costs. This rfow is not actually part of the cash flow forecast, but it helps to keep the level of sales in mind.

Before you can complete the forecast you need to estimate the length of time it will take to collect money from your customers (typically at least 30 days from issuing an invoice) and to settle with your creditors. If you are registered for VAT, it will help to show it separately.

Grants and loans

Grants should not need to be repaid, loans obviously will.

Other

Include also any additional cash, savings, etc which you put into the business.

Payments

Your payments will include those made to cover general business costs and any other significant cash outflows, eg large purchases and charges.

Costs

These will include those costs which are fixed for the business for a reasonable length of time, for example rent, salaries, etc and those which are related to production levels, for example cost of raw materials to manufacture the product. They will include some or all of the following:

a) Employees' wages and NI

b) Your own drawings from the business

c) Rent

d) Rates

e) Insurance

f) Advertising and promotion

g) Bank charges

h) Interest on and repayment of loans

i) Admin costs, telephone, stationery, etc

j) Raw materials

k) Power supply

l) Packaging

m) Transport

n) Consumable goods, such as fuel

o) Repairs and renewals.

Taxation

If you are registered for VAT, then potential receipts and payments should be shown. If you operate as a limited company and pay corporation tax on chargeable profits, you should include this also. Ask your accountant or business counsellor for advice.

Professional fees

These may be a fixed cost, for example for regular accounting or auditing fees, or may arise unexpectedly, eg legal advice.

Capital purchases

If you expect to spend large sums on capital equipment (ie items which you can reasonably expect to last more than 12 months), then you need to determine cost and likely timing for these purchases. Any hire purchase and leasing payments also need to be recorded.

Not all of the costs listed will apply to every business, and there may be costs associated with your business which are not mentioned. Try to ensure that you list all those items which apply to you.

Preparing the cash flow

As shown earlier, the cash flow forecast is set out as a table, with receipts and payments set against the months in which they occur. If you are not yet trading, show figures from the month in which you plan to start up. As a general rule, when completing the cash flow:

i) First fill in your predictable payments. This will be simple for those made monthly; for others, eg advertising costs, try to predict as far as possible when they will occur.

ii) Now consider probable sales receipts, remembering to allow for seasonal variations, if these affect your business.

iii) Once you have a sales forecast you can start to fill in your direct costs, which are related to levels of sales and production.

iv) List all items separately, and in the month in which the money will be paid into your business or will be expended by it.

v) Round all figures up or down to avoid over complicating the financial picture.

Using the cash flow

Once you have completed the forecast entries as far as possible, you can calculate total receipts and payments month by month. You can then work out the cash flow for each month and your cumulative balance (ie money in the bank):

Total monthly receipts − total monthly payments = monthly balance

Include the forecast bank balance at the start of the month (nil if this is the opening cash flow) and at the end of the month. Your overall balance may be positive or negative, depending on how much cash has been going in or out of the business. At start-up, it is likely to be negative for some time, but the forecast should allow you to predict when growth will occur.

The forecast can now be used to determine:

i)   How much cash the business needs in order to be viable

ii) When you might need an injection of cash

iii) The personal income (drawings) you can allow yourself from the business.

USEFUL TIPS

● *Be cautious, especially at start-up, about anticipating cash inflows. In reality, cash tends to go out from the business more quickly than it comes in.*

● *Businesses seeking significant investment may wish to undertake three year forecasts. The first year cash flow is usually shown monthly, the second year quarterly and the third year as a single figure.*

8 Understanding balance sheets

This section explains the key information found in a balance sheet.

Introduction

A balance sheet is a financial 'snapshot' which summarises the assets and liabilities of a business at a specific point in time. All businesses have to prepare a balance sheet at least once each year, as part of their annual accounts, but a balance sheet can be prepared at any time.

The balance sheet shows:

i)   How much capital is employed in the business.

ii) How quickly assets can be turned into cash.

iii) How solvent the business is.

iv) How the business is financed.

Balance sheet at 30.4.95

	£	£
Fixed assets		
Tangible assets		
Equipment	40,000	
Buildings	95,000	
Intangible assets		
Goodwill	5,000	140,000
Current assets		
Stock	10,000	
Debtors	20,000	
Cash at bank	5,000	
		35,000
Current liabilities		
Overdraft		
Loans	23,000	
Creditors	7,000	
Tax	2,000	
		32,000
Net current assets		3,000
Total assets less current liabilities		143,000
Creditors: falling due after one year		100,000
Net assets		43,000
Capital and reserves		
Shareholders		30,000
Reserves		13,000
Net worth		43,000

In reading a balance sheet, it is important to remember (at least from the accounting point of view) that the owner of the business and the business are separate entities. Thus if you invest £20,000 to start your own business, the business 'owes' you £20,000. In other words, the assets (£20,000, say, in the bank) are exactly matched by the liabilities. This must always be the case – otherwise the balance sheet would not balance.

It is also important to remember what a balance sheet is not:

i)   It does *not* show the profitability of a business; this is demonstrated in the profit and loss account.

ii)   It does *not* show the value of a business; this depends on profitability and the current values (as opposed to costs) of assets.

There are a number of different ways of setting out a balance sheet. It has been traditional to set out a balance sheet horizontally, with the liabilities on the left and the assets on the right. In this case, the liabilities include the money invested in the business. In other words, the total liabilities are equal to the total capital employed. For the non-accountant this is not always easy to read or to interpret quickly. It is becoming increasingly common, therefore, for balance sheets to be laid out in a vertical format, as shown in the example on page 80.

Key terms

Fixed assets

Fixed assets are generally assets with a life longer than one year, such as equipment and buildings. These are also known as tangible assets because they physically exist. There is also a class of fixed assets known as intangible assets. Goodwill, for example, is an intangible asset. If you buy a business for more than its net worth, the difference is shown on the balance sheet as goodwill. This is a representation of your expectation of future earning power. Since you can never be sure of recouping goodwill if you wish to sell, it is good practice to write off (depreciate) goodwill as quickly as possible.

The cost of tangible fixed assets is also depreciated over the expected lives of the assets; it is quite common to see the original cost of tangible assets together with their accumulated depreciation on a balance sheet.

Current assets and current liabilities

Current assets and current liabilities usually have a life of less than one year. Current assets include stock, work in progress, debtors, cash at bank, etc. Debtors represents the amount of money owed to you by customers. Current liabilities include overdrafts, loans due within one year, money owed under hire purchase agreements, any amounts owed in VAT or tax, etc. Creditors represents the amount of money owed by you to suppliers.

Net current assets is simply the difference between current assets and current liabilities. This should be positive, otherwise you may not be able to meet your debts as they fall due. If so, then you may be insolvent. In retail businesses, however, because there are no trade debtors, there are often net current liabilities.

Net assets

The example shows the creditors falling due after more than one year deducted to give the net assets. This will probably only include bank loans and HP payments due in more than 12 months. Deducting this figure from the net current assets gives the net assets of the business.

Capital employed

Some accountants include long term loans with the capital and reserves. Adding the two together gives the capital employed. A small business, with little or no long term loans, but a higher level of short term loans, should include all loans in capital employed.

Net worth

The net assets should be equal to the total capital and reserves, that is, the net worth. This comprises the money introduced by the shareholders or owners and the reserves. Normally, the reserves are simply the retained profits. The capital and reserves is sometimes known as the 'equity' of the business.

In the example:

The total assets are £175,000.

The capital employed, equal to capital and reserves plus long term loan also equal to the total assets less current liabilities is £143,000.

The net worth is £43,000 (ie total assets less current liabilities, less long term debt; equal to shareholders' capital plus reserves).

Net assets are £43,000, ie total assets less current liabilities and long term debt.

USEFUL TIPS

● *If you require assistance to draw up balance sheets you could use an accountant or contact a business counsellor at your local enterprise agency.*

● *All of the information required to write up a basic balance sheet can be obtained from a trial balance, which is a summary of your accounting books and records.*

9 Understanding profit and loss accounts

Introduction

A profit and loss account (P&L) shows what happened in a business, in terms of income, sales and expenditure, during a specific period. All businesses have to prepare a profit and loss account at least once each year, as part of the annual accounts. In that case the P&L covers a year's activities. However, they can be prepared for a period of any length.

The P&L shows:

i) The turnover or sales for the period.

ii) The expenditure for the period.

iii) How much profit there was.

iv) How the profit has been divided.

Profit and loss accounts are generally set out in the way illustrated in the example overleaf.

Profit and loss account for the year ending 30.4.95.

	£	£
Sales 2000 units @£100		£200,000
Less direct costs		
Raw materials	60,000	
Sub-contract	20,000	80,000
Gross profit		120,000
Overhead costs		
Employee wages	40,000	
Premises costs	11,000	
Advertising	9,000	
Transport	7,000	
Office costs	5,000	
Bank charges	1,000	
Interest on loan	5,000	
Depreciation	10,000	
Total overheads		88,000
Net profit before appropriations		32,000
Less: drawings		20,000
Tax		7,000
Retained in business		5,000

Key terms

Sales figure

The sales figure shows the actual sales for the period, excluding VAT. It does not reflect the cash received from customers since some payments may still be outstanding. A basic principle in accounting is to match costs against the revenues generated by those costs, so it is important that the sales figure is correctly calculated. It should be the sum of all invoices issued during the period.

Direct costs

The direct costs, that is, those costs directly attributable to the sales, reflect raw materials and sub-contract costs in the product or service actually sold during the period. In some businesses, employee costs can also be directly attributed to the product sold.

There may be stock purchased during the period which was not consumed; this will be shown on the balance sheet but not charged to the profit and loss account. Conversely, raw materials may have been consumed which were bought in a previous period. The cost of those materials will be included in the direct costs. Materials purchased but not consumed will be shown in the stock figure on the balance sheet.

You need to watch out for purchases of materials or sub-contract work which have gone into sales made during the period, but for which you have not been billed. Ideally, you will not prepare the accounts until all bills have been received. However, when producing management accounts you may need to make an estimate of these costs to give a profit figure which is as accurate as possible.

Profit

The direct costs are deducted from the sales figure to give gross profit. This allows you to calculate your gross profit margin. The overheads are deducted from the gross profit to give the net profit.

Keep an eye on both your gross profit margin and your net profit margin (60% and 16% in the example). Dramatic reductions in either could be a sign of trouble.

Depreciation

One element in the P&L does not involve a movement of cash. This is depreciation. Depreciation is charged to cover the wear and tear of fixed assets. The amount charged therefore is an allocation of the cost of fixed assets over their useful life. This is often charged at the rate of 25% of capital cost per year. If depreciation is high relative to payroll costs you have a capital intensive business; if the payroll costs are high relative to depreciation, you have a labour intensive business.

Appropriation account

It is usual at the bottom of a P&L account to show an 'appropriation account', that is, an explanation of how the profit is divided. Profit can be divided in just three ways: to the shareholders or owners (as dividends or drawings); to the government as tax; or, it might be retained in the business (to use as working capital or to buy equipment or other assets).

USEFUL TIPS

- *If you are worried about excessive overhead charges, it is useful to refer to the P&L as it gives a breakdown of each individual type of expense.*

- *By drawing up a P&L you will be able to see whether corrective action is needed to maximise profit. For example, you may discover the percentage of raw materials as a proportion of sales is too high.*

- *If you are unsure of how to draw up a P&L you could use an accountant, or contact a business counsellor at your local enterprise agency.*

10 Financial ratios

This section explains some of the key indicators used by businesses to assess their performance.

Background

It is often difficult to look at a profit and loss account or a balance sheet and derive a full picture. As a result, ratios are often used to interpret accounts. A ratio is simply a relationship between two numbers. When compared to the same ratios in the accounts for previous periods, trends and patterns of performance can be seen. They can also be compared with the same ratios for other businesses operating in a similar environment – giving an idea of relative performance. Ratios are published for many business sectors which can be used as a comparison (these are sometimes referred to as 'Industry Norms').

This section looks briefly at four different types of ratio:

i)   Liquidity – the amount of working capital available.

ii) Solvency – how near is the business to bankruptcy.

iii) Efficiency – how good is the management.

iv) Profitability – how good is the business as an investment.

Liquidity ratios

A business should always have enough current assets (eg stock, work in progress, debtors, cash in the bank, etc) to cover current liabilities (eg bank overdraft, creditors, etc). Liquidity ratios indicate the ability to meet liabilities with the assets available. The current ratio shows the relationship of current assets to current liabilities.

$$\text{Current ratio} = \frac{\text{Current assets}}{\text{Current liabilities}}$$

This ratio should normally be between 1.5 and 2. Some people argue that the current ratio should be at least 2 on the basis that half the assets might be stock. If it is less than 1 (ie current liabilities exceed current assets) you could be insolvent. A stricter test of liquidity is the quick ratio or acid test. Some current assets, such as work in progress and stock, may be difficult to turn quickly into cash. Deducting these from the current assets gives the quick assets.

$$\text{Quick ratio} = \frac{\text{Quick assets}}{\text{Current liabilities}}$$

The quick ratio should normally be around 0.7-1. To be absolutely safe, the quick ratio should be at least 1, which indicates that quick assets exceed current liabilities. If the current ratio is rising and the quick ratio is static, there is almost certainly a stockholding problem.

Some people find it helpful to calculate the 'defensive interval'. This is the best measure of impending insolvency and shows the number of days the business can exist if no more cash flows into the business. As a guide, it should be 30-90 days, though it depends on your industry.

$$\text{Defensive interval (days)} = \frac{\text{Quick assets}}{\text{Daily operating expenses}}$$

Solvency ratios

If the net worth of the business becomes negative, ie the total liabilities exceed total assets, then the business has become insolvent. That is, if the business closed it would not be possible to repay all the people who are owed money. Allowing a company to become insolvent is an offence, so you should take care to watch the figures closely.

One ratio which gives an indication of solvency is the gearing. It is normally defined as the ratio of debt (ie loans from all sources including debentures, term loans and overdraft) to total finance (ie shareholders' capital plus reserves plus long-term debt plus overdraft). The higher the proportion of loan finance, the higher the gearing.

$$\text{Gearing} = \frac{\text{Loans} + \text{bank overdraft}}{\text{Equity} + \text{loans} + \text{bank overdraft}}$$

The gearing should not be greater than 50% although it often is for new, small businesses. If cashflow is stable and profit is fairly stable, then you can afford a higher gearing.

In addition to watching the gearing, bankers will also want to be satisfied that you will be able to pay the interest on their loans. They particularly look, therefore, at how many times your profit exceeds their interest.

$$\text{Interest cover} = \frac{\text{Profit before}}{\text{interest and tax (PBIT)}}$$

If this is more than 4 it is very good. If it is less than 2 it may indicate potential problems if interest rates rise.

Efficiency ratios

Efficiency ratios provide a measure of how much working capital is tied up, indicate how quickly you collect outstanding debts (and pay your creditors) and show how effective you are in making your money work for you.

$$\text{Debtors' turnover ratio} = \frac{\text{Sales (incl. VAT)}}{\text{Debtors}}$$

Ideally use the average debtors for the period. An approximation is given by dividing the sales by the debtors at the end of the period. Dividing this ratio into the days of the year gives the average collection period in days.

$$\text{Average collection period} = \frac{365 \times \text{Debtors}}{\text{Sales}}$$

Tight credit control is essential. Keep the collection period as short as possible. Many businesses aim to operate on 30 days, but often find it is worse than that.

Monitoring how long it takes to pay your suppliers is as important as knowing how long your customers take to pay you. If suppliers have to wait too long, they may withdraw credit facilities.

$$\text{Creditors' turnover ratio} = \frac{\text{Cost of sales}}{\text{Creditors}}$$

$$\text{Average payment period} = \frac{365 \times \text{Creditors}}{\text{Cost of sales}}$$

It is normal to use cost of sales in calculating the average payment period. When comparing your business with others, however, you may need to approximate by using the sales figure, unless you can determine the cost of sales of your competitors.

Stock will increase in times of expansion and decrease in times of contraction. For some businesses, such as wholesalers and some retailers, a high stock turnover ratio is essential in order to make any profit. A low stock turnover could indicate the presence of slow moving stock, which should be disposed of rapidly.

$$\text{Stock turnover ratio} = \frac{\text{Cost of sales}}{\text{Stock level}}$$

It is often helpful to know how quickly the stock is turned over.

$$\text{Average holding period} = \frac{365 \times \text{Stock}}{\text{Cost of sales}}$$

Dell Computer Corporation, for example, aims for a stock holding period of just 11 days.

Profitability ratios

There are a number of simple profitability indicators that you can use. The gross profit margin is one figure to watch closely.

$$\text{Gross profit margin} = \frac{\text{Gross profit}}{\text{Sales}} \times 100\%$$

You should also monitor the net profit margin.

$$\text{Net profit margin} = \frac{\text{PBIT}}{\text{Sales}} \times 100\%$$

Some funders will want to know the return on the capital employed. This will give a comparison with what could have been achieved had the same sum of money been put in a building society or invested on the stock market.

$$\text{Net profit margin} = \frac{\text{PBIT}}{\text{Total capital employed}} \times 100\%$$

- *The key use of ratios is to examine trends and identify problems. Ratios will never solve problems but they might help to lead you to the cause.*

- *The smaller the business the more important it is to watch the cashflow, rather than relying on ratio analysis.*

- *Ratios depend upon accurate, consistent financial information.*

- *Ratios are normally judged against the industry norms and against the business' own performance record; they can tell you little in isolation.*

Capital
investment

part
four

11 Investment appraisal

Using payback and accounting rate of return techniques

This section looks at how the potential returns offered to an investor by different investments may be compared using the techniques of payback and accounting rate of return (also known as return on capital employed).

Introduction

Anyone investing money, either for themselves or on behalf of a business, has to consider their options. They should take into account the potential returns of each option, and the associated risks, before making a decision. When comparing the returns from different investment options, a number of techniques are available.

When you make a capital investment, you do so because you expect to generate income in the future. If this were not the case, you would not make the investment. So you need to compare cash outflows now with the likely cash inflows at some time in the future.

If your capital investments are relatively small, it is unlikely that you will need or want to use special techniques to appraise them. Larger investments should, however, be looked at closely. Do the benefits of the investment exceed the costs? For example, are you making a sufficient return on your investment?

Decisions about major investments need to be made carefully because large sums of money will often be involved. Once a decision has been implemented it will be difficult to reverse.

A comprehensive evaluation will allow for taxation, inflation, etc and for the risk that your estimates are inaccurate. As so often in business, the greatest difficulty is in estimating likely sales at the price you expect to charge over the life of the investment. You will have to estimate the useful life of the assets, the cost of maintenance, any effect (positive or negative) on other aspects of your work, additional working capital required particularly if you are forecasting increased sales, etc.

There are a number of ways of assessing whether you should invest in a particular project. The objective of every technique is to help you decide whether the return on capital you will make is sufficient to make the project attractive. For larger businesses, this becomes a very simple exercise which compares the returns available from different opportunities. For smaller businesses, there are intangible returns. For example, failure to invest may threaten the future of the business. Jobs, particularly of the principals, may be at stake. Logically, if business proprietors cannot get a sufficient return, then they should work for someone else and invest their money in a different way. Practically, they may not be able to get a job elsewhere, or may not want to, and so this needs to be taken into account.

There are effectively two approaches to capital appraisal. Non-surplus methods use guesswork or intuition. Surplus methods assess whether there is a surplus of benefit over cost in order to decide whether funds should be allocated to a particular project.

The very simplest surplus method uses the ratio of total revenue to total expenditure. If the ratio is greater than one, proceed. This ignores both time and the cost of funds. More sophisticated techniques take such factors into account. This section looks at the techniques of payback and accounting rate of return.

Payback

The payback method looks at how long it takes for a business to recover its initial investment. How long will it take before the cost savings or increased income repay the initial investment? The best way to understand the calculation is to follow the example below:

Barry's Boards is a business which primarily offers design and manufacture of printed circuit boards, supplying manufacturers of electronic equipment. He works with the manufacturer's product designers to develop a specification for each new board, then completes the circuit layout design. Once a prototype has been tested and approved, he manufactures the required quantity. He is considering spending £65,000 on new board etching equipment so that he can take on bigger and more complex production runs.

He has looked carefully at the total costs involved and estimated the additional income that he is likely to generate as a direct result. He has then calculated the net operating profit for each of the next five years.

Barry's Boards

Year	Cash flow	Net position
0	(65,000)	(65,000)
1	2,000	(63,000)
2	7,500	(55,500)
3	20,500	(35,000)
4	33,000	(2,000)
5	45,000	43,000

He plots the cash flows on a bar chart, as shown in the dark shading in the figure. He has also plotted the cumulative position (in light shading) which shows that the machine will have paid for itself in just over four years (excluding interest payments on any loan used for the purchase).

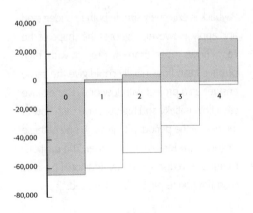

The example looked at a manufacturing business, but it could just as easily have been, for example, an industrial design business investing £65,000 in new hardware and CAD software; or a business considering an investment in a research and development (R&D) project. In all cases, estimating the income associated with the project is difficult, but it is at least relatively easy to estimate the cost, which is normally required up-front. In the R&D case, whilst the principles are exactly the same, the cost can often be as hard to estimate as the income. Furthermore, the costs may be incurred over months or even years before the investment starts to generate an income. Other appraisal techniques may, therefore, be preferable, particularly for the R&D case.

Payback is extremely simple both to understand and apply. However, it ignores the shape of the cash flows over time. A project with high positive cash flow initially could give the same answer as a project with low or even negative cash flow initially and high positive cash flow at the end of the period, yet intuitively one of these might be preferable to the other. The payback method also disregards any additional positive cash flow once payback is achieved.

Note that depreciation should be ignored completely since it does not represent a movement of cash, but you will need to include the cost of the finance when calculating the total payments.

Accounting rate of return

Some businesses look at the accounting rate of return over the likely life of the asset or for a specific period, sometimes known as the accounting rate of return.

Looking again at the example of Barry's Boards: the project generates a net profit of £108,000 over five years, that is, an average of £21,600 per annum. Barry's total outlay, that is the capital employed, is £65,000. Strictly speaking, you should use average capital employed for the period, but it is suggested that you simply use the capital employed figure. In this case, the return is 33% (that is the average profit of £21,600 divided by capital employed of £65,000 and the result multiplied by 100). If the cost of borrowing the money, or the opportunity cost, is less than 33% then this is a project worth pursuing.

If you choose to use average capital employed, you will need also to take into account any residual value for the equipment (that is, the sum which may be obtained if the equipment were sold. If we assume a residual value of £6,000, then the average capital employed is £35,500 (that is, the opening capital employed of £65,000 plus the closing capital employed of £6,000 divided by two), so the return on capital employed is 61%.

Since the entire investment has to be found at the beginning of the period, many people prefer to use the initial investment figure as the capital employed. This gives a lower figure for the return on investment, but arguably one that is more realistic.

The example implies that the expenditure is a one off event, after which cash flow becomes positive. If the expenditure is incurred over months or years, as in the case of investing in research and development, you will need to use the total project period, rather than the periods for which cash flow is positive, in calculating the average annual profit and, therefore, the average annual return.

Although this method gives some idea of the return on the investment and consequently a way of assessing a margin of error, it still does not take into account the shape of the cash flows over time. It begs the question of whether simply to use the figure for capital employed at the start of the period or to use the figure for average capital employed during the period. By itself, it cannot be used to rank different opportunities if they have different time frames.

USEFUL TIPS

- *Before starting your appraisal, think carefully about the criteria for choosing whether or not to proceed. Do not do the calculation and then bend the criteria to fit.*

- *Prepare detailed cash flow forecasts, as accurately as you can, for the life of the project or, for payback calculations, for a period long enough to achieve payback.*

12 Investment appraisal

Using discounted cash flow techniques

This section looks at how the potential returns offered to an investor by different investments may be compared using the discounted cash flow (DCF) techniques of net present value (NPV) and internal rate of return (IRR).

Introduction

Anyone with money to invest, either for themselves or on behalf of a business, should consider the options open to them. Ideally they will take into account the potential returns of each option, and the associated risks, before a decision is made. When comparing the returns from different investment options, a number of techniques are available. Discounted cash flow techniques are discussed here.

The techniques of payback and accounting rate of return have disadvantages; neither allows for the cost of the money (interest, arrangement fees, etc) or the fact that a pound in your hand now is worth more than a pound in, say, one year's time. For a more accurate appraisal, you should use a discounted cash flow technique such as net present value or internal rate of return. This section explains the concept of discounting and then goes on to explain the appraisal techniques.

Discounting

£100 in your hand now is not the same as £100 receivable in one year because the money you have now could be earning interest. If the current rate of interest is 10%, then the money you hold now will be worth £110 in one year. If this were reinvested, it would be worth £121 after a further year. This is known as compounding and can be calculated as follows:

£100 now will be worth £100 multiplied by $(1 + r)$ in one year; £100 x $(1 + r)^2$ in two years and £100 x $(1 + r)^n$ where n is the number of years and r is the current rate of interest expressed as a decimal (for example, 15% is calculated using $0.15)^3$.

This means that £100 with interest at 15% compounded over three years calculates as:

£100 x $(1 + 0.15)^3$ which equals £152.08

In the reverse case, you might want to know what £100 receivable in n years is worth now. At an interest rate of 10%, £100 receivable in one year is worth: 100 divided by $(1 + 0.1) =$ £91 now; £100 receivable in two years is worth $100/(1.1)^2 = £83$ now.

In other words, if you were given £83 now and invested it for two years at 10%, it would by then be worth £100. This procedure is the opposite of compounding and is called discounting.

Generally, we can say that: £1 receivable in n years is worth $1/(1+r)^n$. The result of the calculation is known as the discount factor.

A discounted cash flow shows future cash flows, usually over several years, adjusted by a suitable discount factor, to take account of the timing of the cash flow. Discounting to the present day gives the net present value (NPV). Using the above example, at an interest rate of 10%, £100 receivable in two years has a net present value of £83.

Net present value

One method of comparing different options is to consider the net present value of each. Provided you have chosen an appropriate interest rate, an investment with a net present value which is positive is worth pursuing. If a choice between investments has to be made, the one with the highest NPV is the more profitable.

The first step in calculating NPV is to estimate the cash flows, both positive and negative, for the expected life of the project. This could be expenditure on a CAD system for a service business, or on plant for a manufacturing business, or the total cost of an R & D project, together with the income expected to arise from that expenditure. The net cash flow is usually shown as the net profit, ignoring interest and tax and depreciation, which does not represent a movement of cash. The capital expenditure is usually shown in Year 0 (see table opposite), though this would clearly be different where cash is expended over a period of months or years. These cash flows then need to be discounted to present values at a predetermined rate of interest. This is often taken as the cost of capital to your business, particularly appropriate if you will need to borrow the money from the bank. If you already have the money available, then it may be more appropriate to use the opportunity cost, that is, the rate of return you could achieve if you invested the money elsewhere, for example in a deposit account.

Here is an example of investment appraisal using NPV:

Barry's Boards is a business which primarily offers design and manufacture of printed circuit boards, supplying manufacturers of electronic equipment. He works with the manufacturer's product designers to develop a specification for each new board, then completes the circuit layout design. Once a prototype has been tested and approved, he manufactures the required quantity. He is considering spending £65,000 on new board etching equipment so that he can take on bigger and more complex production runs. Barry has estimated the net cash flows as shown in the table below. Note that he expects to generate income for five years, and has used an interest rate of 8% to calculate the discount factors.

Year value	Cash flow	Discount factor	Present
0	(65,000)	1.000	(65,000)
1	2,000	.9259	1,852
2	7,500	.8573	6,430
3	20,500	.7938	16,273
4	33,000	.7350	24,255
5	45,000	.6806	30,627
NPV			14,437

The cash flows are multiplied by the discount factor to give the present values. These are totalled to give the net present value. In this case, the NPV is £14,437; this is positive so the return is greater than 8%. In other words, the project is worth pursuing.

Suppose Barry has to borrow the money and has been offered a loan at an interest rate of 16%. He now does the calculation again using different discount factors.

Year value	Cash flow	Discount factor	Present
0	(65,000)	1.000	(65,000)
1	2,000	.8621	1,724
2	7,500	.7432	5,574
3	20,500	.6407	13,134
4	33,000	.5523	18,226
5	45,000	.4761	21,424
NPV			(4,918)

This time the NPV is negative. The project returns less than it costs to borrow the money so it is not worth doing purely in financial terms.

As with any cash flow forecasting, there are bound to be errors in the forecasts. It is difficult to forecast sales a few months ahead, let alone years. It can be difficult to allocate a fair proportion of overheads to a single machine or a single service or a particular piece of research and development; this is essential if the answer is going to be anywhere close to accurate.

This technique can be used to compare the returns on different projects or on different ways of implementing the same project. For example, is it cheaper to borrow the money to buy equipment outright, or to lease the equipment?

Internal rate of return

An alternative to calculating net present value is to calculate the internal rate of return (IRR). This is the estimated annual percentage return on the initial investment, once again allowing for the fact that future receipts are worth less than receipts today. With NPV you use a pre-determined rate of return. Calculating the IRR tells you the rate of return for a project.

The IRR is, simply, the discount rate which gives an NPV of zero. It is, if you like, the real rate of return. It is the same as the figure which lenders quote as the annual percentage rate (APR). It can be compared to the cost of the capital or, in larger businesses, often to a predefined threshold. If it is higher than the cost of capital or the threshold, the investment is worth pursuing; an investment with a higher IRR is more profitable. Uncertainty also needs to be considered. The more risky a project, the higher IRR you will be seeking to compensate for the risk, but your assumptions may be less certain. You might, therefore, choose a lower level of risk and accept a lower IRR.

Calculating the IRR is normally used by larger companies, who need to know the precise yield, and who have a minimum threshold below which they will not accept projects. If you ever decide to seek equity from a venture capital fund, they will use IRR calculations to help decide whether to invest. They normally have a pre-determined threshold which may be 35% or higher.

You can determine the IRR by calculating NPVs at different rates of interest, as in the example above, and then interpolate or draw a graph to show the interest rate for an NPV of zero. Alternatively, most computerised spreadsheet packages will quickly calculate IRR for you.

Assessing risk

Before you finally go ahead with any major purchase it makes sense to undertake an overall assessment of the likely risk. As part of the planning process you will have already considered all the costs and all the income associated with the initiative. The appraisal technique chosen will depend on the size of the investment, the amount of capital available and whether it has to be borrowed, etc. It probably makes sense to determine in advance the criteria for accepting an investment. Using IRR means that you can compare the result with the cost of the investment – but that still leaves the problem of how much margin you should leave to allow for the different risks involved.

Think about the sensitivity of your forecast to possible changes. What happens if costs rise or sales fall? What effect will that have on profitability? If you are borrowing the money, what is the effect on your gearing and interest cover? Will the bank still be happy? You may want to look at the internal rate of return for the worst scenario as well as the most likely scenario. If this is still above your target return, well and good. If it is below, you need to think carefully about the different risks and the steps that can be taken to mitigate them. What can you do to increase the chances of achieving your sales forecast or of ensuring costs do not rise more than forecast?

- *Before starting your appraisal, think carefully about the criteria for choosing whether to proceed, including any risk premium.*

- *Prepare detailed cash flow forecasts, as accurately as you can, for the life of the project.*

Finding
capital

part
five

13 Financing a business

This section reviews the different methods of financing a business and how funds raised are matched to business needs.

Introduction

Whether you are starting up or expanding a business you will have a number of financial requirements. Unless you are very lucky there will be a gap between paying your suppliers and receiving payment from your own customers. Customers will delay payment for as long as they can; this may be for as long as three or four months. You may find it more difficult to persuade your suppliers to wait as long for payment and hence you will need 'working capital'. In addition, you may need to buy or lease equipment and premises. These too will need to be financed.

There are three possible sources of money though two of them can be sub-divided:

Equity

You might provide it, say from your savings, or you might persuade acquaintances or financial institutions to invest in the business.

Grants (quasi-equity)

A grant may be available from the government, your local authority or a related organisation.

Loans

You might persuade a bank or some other lender to provide a loan to the business.

Creditors

You might 'borrow' from your trade creditors, though this is often difficult until the business has built up a good credit record.

Profits

If you are already in business, you may be able to retain some of the profit within the business. This becomes part of the equity in the business but it is also available to help fund working capital or additional fixed assets.

In general, banks and other lenders aim to match the term of a loan to the expected useful life of an asset, though they 'play safe' with the loan term being shorter.

Business finance is often divided into three categories:

i)   Short term: trade creditors and overdraft.

ii) Medium term: loans of less than seven years, leasing and hire purchase.

iii) Long term: loans of more than seven years and equity.

Funding working capital

Unless there is sufficient equity in the business (whether introduced as capital invested or as retained profit), working capital is generally funded by trade creditors and an overdraft facility. The disadvantage of an overdraft is that it is repayable on demand. You will also have to pay an arrangement fee, but you will only pay interest on the outstanding balance. Whilst the interest rate may be higher than for a term loan the overall cost may be lower. The bank may also seek a personal guarantee and/or a charge over assets. The size of overdraft required clearly depends on the working capital requirement and has to be agreed at least annually with your bank manager.

The current assets less the current liabilities shown on the balance sheet are the business's working capital. The balance sheet though is only a snapshot of the business. Your cash flow forecast, therefore, gives a more accurate figure. Even this, however, is prone to error. Receipts may be delayed by two or three weeks, pushing up the requirement in the middle of a month, for example, though this will not be reflected in month end figures.

Some businesses, such as retail or mail order, are cash positive. In other words, they receive cash for their goods straight away but do not have to pay their creditors for 30, 60 or 90 days. These businesses can easily fund their working capital solely from trade creditors. For most businesses, customer payments will be made after supplier invoices become due. As a rule of thumb, it makes sense to aim for minimum working capital of a month's average sales multiplied by the number of months it takes to collect payment. If you want to be more accurate, then use the following procedure (shown with example):

Determine average number of weeks raw material is in stock	2
Deduct: credit period from suppliers in weeks	(-4)
Add: average number of weeks to produce goods or service	1
Add: average number of weeks finished goods are in stock	1
Add: average time customers take to pay	9
Total	**9**

If sales for the year are estimated at £208,000 then the maximum working capital required is 9/52 x 208,000 = £36,000. It would be more accurate to use the cost of sales (direct and fixed) rather than the full selling price, but the above will give a sufficient approximation. If your business is growing, then your overdraft requirement will grow at the same rate.

An alternative method of financing working capital, at least in part, is factoring or invoice discounting. There are a number of factoring agents who will take your invoices and give you a proportion of the total, around 80%, immediately. The balance is paid (less their commission) when the customer pays the factor. Factoring is therefore an expensive way of speeding up cash flow for small businesses, but larger businesses may reduce their administration costs by this method. Generally, factoring agents expect businesses to have sales of at least £30,000 per month.

Funding capital assets

Capital assets are usually defined by their life and divided into medium and long term finance. Equipment and machinery is usually financed over three years. Agreements should ideally be over the life of the asset but most banks will exercise caution. In the case of buildings which have a long life, say 60 years plus, long term finance in the form of a mortgage may be available.

Equity, or shareholder capital, is the money introduced into a business by the proprietor(s) and anyone else willing to invest capital in the hope of getting a future return. If it is a company, then the equity is introduced in exchange for shares. If the business does well, the directors declare a dividend each year. If it does very well, it may be floated on the Alternative Investment Market or the Stock Market, in which case the original share holdings will become valuable. Often though, shareholders' capital will be locked into the small business. Corporation tax is payable on all profits. Dividends, if paid, are distributed from post tax profit.

Loan capital, or debt, is money lent to a business. Normally, the period of the loan is determined according to the life of the asset for which it is used. A long term loan for premises and a medium or short term loan for equipment. Interest on loans is tax deductible, whereas dividends are paid out of profit. The purchase of buildings or land can probably be spread over 20 or 25 years with the asset used as security for the loan. It is unusual however for the banks to provide the entire sum required, preferring to limit their loan to 75% of the value of the assets.

Once you have built up a track record with your bank, you should be able to attract medium term loans, say three to seven years, to cover the cost of the plant and equipment. Established companies may be able to raise long term debt as a debenture or convertible loan stock which normally receives a fixed rate of interest and is repayable in full at the end of the term. Debentures sometimes carry options to turn them into shares. Long term debt is usually included with the capital on the balance sheet, whereas short term debt, and especially overdrafts, are treated as current liabilities.

Most banks look for a gearing of about one to one. The gearing is the proportion of debt to total finance; the higher the gearing, the more debt there is relative to equity. Once your business starts to grow, therefore, it will be essential to introduce more money as equity or else retain substantial profits in the business.

It is often possible for businesses to buy equipment on hire purchase, leasing or lease purchasing. Lease companies will not have the same concerns about gearing as the banks. They will, however, be interested in your cash flow and whether you can afford the repayments. The equipment will remain the property of the leasing company; you have the legal right to use the equipment for the period of the lease assuming, of course, that the lease payments are up to date. At the end of the lease, the equipment reverts to the leasing company, although it is often possible to buy the equipment for a small sum.

Grants

There are several sources of grant aid which should be investigated when you are starting in business and, particularly, whenever you are buying equipment. At the least, check with the Department of Trade and Industry locally and with your local authority to see if they have any grants available for which you might qualify.

- *Keep your lenders informed of your financial position; giving ample warning if you wish to increase your overdraft, for example.*

- *In times of recession, try to keep as much of your debt as possible as fixed medium term loans and keep your overdraft requirement to the minimum. In times of expansion, when finance is more readily available, it may be more cost effective to use an overdraft.*

14 Sources of small business finance

This section gives an overview of the types of finance available to small businesses, together with some of the most likely sources.

Introduction

There are three sources of funds for any business – equity, loans and retained earnings. Most businesses rely largely on loan finance, obtaining loans and overdrafts from the major banks. As commercial lenders, the banks are concerned with getting a good return on their investments and do not want to lose their investors' money on businesses that go bankrupt. Banks are increasingly responsive to the needs of small businesses, but there are many occasions where the risk of lending is considered too high. This is usually because the business is being started by someone with little previous business experience and not much of their own capital to invest, and there is insufficient security.

Small businesses often need other sources of financial help if they are to grow and develop. Financial assistance and advice to small businesses is available all over the country, especially in areas of high unemployment and economic deprivation. Funds may come from the government (at EU, national and local level) and from a number of organisations such as Local Enterprise Agencies. Many major private companies collaborate with such organisations to provide finance in the form of grants and loans. Banks are more likely to help small businesses who are receiving support and advice from these agencies.

Small business support networks

The networks of organisations which makes financial support and advice available to small firms seem to be constantly changing. Identifying the right package of support can be complicated. Several regional networks – Business Links (England), Business Shops (Scotland), Business Connects (Wales) and the Local Enterprise Development Unit (LEDU) Regional Offices in Northern Ireland – have all been established to clarify matters. All of these networks provide 'one-stop shops', bringing together information on all the most important local and national business support services for small and medium sized businesses. Every area now has a local Business Link (or equivalent) office. The main services provided by these networks are business information, Personal Business Advisers (PBAs) and a range of more specialised consultancy services. Anyone starting a business or needing further assistance should first contact their local Business Link (or equivalent), which should signpost them to relevant local and national sources of advice and financial assistance. Business Link (or equivalent) services are mostly free or subsidised.

Financial assistance is often provided for specific purposes eg marketing or rent relief; specific types of business eg manufacturing, technology; particular types of people, eg unemployed or young people; or for specific areas eg rural areas or areas of industrial decline. Anyone starting or developing a business and looking for financial assistance must produce a comprehensive business plan, clearly setting out the financial case. PBAs can assist with this and can also refer clients to other agencies for more in-depth advice and training. An experienced Business Adviser will know how best to put together a package of support to suit the needs of small businesses and will guide clients through the application process. So many different types of finance and assistance are available that it is worth looking for relevant programmes which may be relatively under-subscribed.

Types of financial support

Loan funds

Terms and conditions for loan funds are often 'soft' – less stringent than for commercial loans. Interest is often fixed for the period of the loan or charged below bank rates. Less security than a bank would seek is usually required. Repayment periods can be flexible, with repayment 'holidays' usually available. Soft loan funds are often 'revolving' – repayments go back into the main fund. Loans are often only available to businesses that are viable, but cannot raise all the finance required from banks. Most funds require borrowers to be monitored for the period of the loan and some integrate loan finance with advisory schemes. Business Advisers are usually familiar with application procedures and should advise clients on the most suitable loan funds to apply for.

Grants and awards

Grants and awards do not need to be repaid. Grants are usually 'one off' payments providing a percentage of the costs towards specific purposes eg marketing, refurbishing premises, capital equipment. They are rarely available to retail businesses. Many local authorities provide grants to encourage small firms. Awards usually recognise achievement and can be either local or national. Awards bring publicity and prizes in cash or in kind. LiveWIRE runs an annual competition for young entrepreneurs and the DTI runs SMART – the Small Firms Merit Award for Science and Technology for UK firms with less than 50 employees.

Venture capital

Venture capital is a means of financing a growing business where a portion of the share capital or equity is sold in return for a major investment in the business. Whilst some measure of personal control over the business is lost to the new shareholder, the amount of finance gained can be very large indeed. Some schemes combine loan and equity finance. The British Venture Capital Association publishes a list of Venture Capital Funds.

The Enterprise Investment Scheme allows businesses to raise finance from private individuals who can invest up to £150,000 per tax year and will receive tax relief on that sum. Investors previously unconnected to the company can become paid directors. The aim is to encourage 'business angels' – wealthy people with extensive business experience – to provide finance and expertise. Most regions of the UK now have 'business angel' matching services, which encourage local investment and mentoring on a smaller scale. The Local Investment Networking Company (LINC) matches investors with small businesses requiring £10,000 to £250,000 on a national scale and is sponsored by several banks.

There is a network of Midland Equity Funds which can provide equity investments below £150,000.

Sources of financial support

This section is a starting point to sources of business finance and is in no way exhaustive. Business Links, etc should have details on what is available locally.

Business start-up

The Training and Enterprise Councils (TECs) in England and Wales or Local Enterprise Companies (LECs) in Scotland and the LEDU in Northern Ireland, administer a variety of schemes to help support new businesses. Each TEC and LEC uses its own discretion in the way that the scheme is run and conditions vary from place to place. Most schemes include business planning, training and some form of financial support.

Department of Trade and Industry (DTI)

The DTI runs a variety of schemes offering financial help to businesses in areas such as technology, research and development, export, etc.

The Small Firms Loan Guarantee Scheme (SFLGS)

Bank loans usually require some security, which not all small businesses can provide. Through the SFLGS, the government acts as a guarantor to a certain percentage of loans made by banks or other financial institutions to small businesses. The SFLGS is not available if a conventional loan can be obtained. The maximum loan which can be covered is £250,000 for a business which has traded for more than two years; if the business is less than two years old the maximum available is £100,000. There are restrictions on the types of companies eligible for SFLGS. Details are available from most banks.

Young people

a) The Prince's Youth Business Trust (PYBT), or PSYBT in Scotland, assists unemployed young people aged 18-29 to start up in business. PYBT is aimed at disadvantaged young people, who often find it difficult to obtain finance from conventional sources. It operates from regional offices, arranging advice and training as well as grants and loans. Grants are also available for pre-start market testing.

b) Shell LiveWIRE, sponsored by Shell UK Ltd, aims to assist young people who are interested in starting their own business. The LiveWIRE Business Start Up awards provide over £200,000 of cash and in-kind support to owner managers aged 16-30 in their first year of trading. Entrants must provide a comprehensive business plan to their local co-ordinator.

Former industrial areas

British Steel (Industry) Ltd provides assistance in areas affected by the decline in the steel industry. It helps businesses to start up, expand or relocate to the designated areas. Finance can take the form of loans or share capital.

Rural areas

The Rural Development Commission (RDC) provides grants towards the redevelopment of redundant rural buildings for commercial purposes. Advice and training for craft businesses is also available.

Local sources of funding

Most areas have funds available for local businesses, often provided through Local

Authorities, Local Enterprise Agencies, TECs, LECs, etc. There may also be less well publicised independent funds and trusts.

European funding

Various European funding schemes are available to businesses, mainly supporting research and development.

USEFUL TIPS

- *Funding for small businesses is frequently raised most effectively as a package of support from several sources. Backing from one source can inspire the confidence of another. The best way to assemble a suitable package of support is through an experienced Business Adviser acting as an intermediary.*

- *A comprehensive business plan is essential before seeking any financial help. The business plan should contain financial forecasts detailing exactly how much money is required and what it will be used for. Business Advisers and bank managers can advise on business plan preparation.*

● *Financial assistance, especially for business start-ups, is often associated with business skills courses. Undertaking business training not only improves personal skills, but will increase the confidence of potential investors in the business.*

Getting paid

15 Factoring and invoice discounting

Introduction

Factoring and invoice discounting are financial services which assure continuous cash flow for a growing business. This service can be useful to businesses which need to speed up payment of invoices to provide working capital for the business.

How it works

A business approaches a debt factoring agency to apply to use its services. The factor, which may be controlled by a bank, will check the business's credit rating, turnover, and customers, before accepting it as a client. In general, they will only accept business from companies with over £100,000 turnover per year.

Once they have accepted a client they will pay up to 80% of the value of an invoice payment due to the client. The balance – less fees and interest rates – is paid when the invoice payment from the customer is received by the factor.

The factoring agency takes on the responsibility and financial burden of collecting payment from the business's debtors and thus frees the business's managers to focus more on the business's primary operations. The factoring company will charge a market interest rate and a fee depending on the level of service provided.

Services available

A variety of services are available from factoring companies. The main ones: full-service factoring, invoice discounting and export factoring, are outlined below:

Full-service factoring

In full-service factoring (sometimes called managed debt factoring), the factor will assume responsibility for both the sales ledger and credit management. Through a factoring agency, a business can expand their purchasing power without relying on bank credit. As a result, they can buy the goods they need, avoiding the normal delays that occur when opening lines of credit. The range of services available from a factoring agency vary and can be tailored to meet the needs of individual companies. Generally, a client can choose from the following services:

a) Non-recourse factoring – provides 100% cover against bad debt.

b) Recourse factoring – in the event of bad debt the factor will recover any advances from the client. The client can take out insurance against bad debt. Some smaller, independent factors do not offer such insurance themselves, but will arrange for this type of protection through a trade credit insurance agency.

c) Confidential factoring – the factor will not disclose the use of its services to a client's customers.

d) Collection of debts either by the factor or by the client on behalf of the factor.

e) Agreement for advance payments either to be based on whole turnover or to be provided for debts as they arise.

f) Flexible finance geared to a business's volume of sales.

Invoice discounting

Invoice discounting is a form of factoring in which the factor lends money to the business against invoices; the business is responsible for collecting the debts itself. In an invoice discounting relationship, the client sends the factoring company a duplicate of all customer invoices sent out. On receipt of the invoice the factor pays the client up to 80% of the value of the invoice. Once the customer has paid the invoice the client repays the amount of the advance, plus fees and interest. In such a relationship the client maintains full control over the sales ledger and is responsible for chasing slow payers.

A business will use invoice discounting when it prefers to keep the involvement of a factoring agency unknown to their customer. Invoice discounting is most often provided by larger factoring agencies because greater sums are involved. It is most suitable for larger companies with a turnover of at least £2million who need finance credit protection but not sales ledger administration. Unlike standard factoring, it generally does not provide for protection against bad debts.

Export factoring

Export factoring is commonly used for companies trying to collect payment from a foreign customer. A factor in the UK, known as an 'export factor', is held responsible for the client's sales ledger and for selecting a factoring agency in the country of the customer. This factor serves as the 'import factor' and is responsible for collecting payment from the customer and passing it on to the export factor.

Factor services can also be provided to overseas companies who are exporting to the UK. Many factors who specialise in financial services for exporting companies offer the following services:

a) Export credit assessment of customers

b) Advice on trading terms in export markets

c) Local collections and assistance with the resolution of disputes

d) Protection against foreign exchange risk

e) Swifter transfer of funds to the UK

f) Expert local knowledge of overseas buyers' credit worthiness

g) Financial facilities available in major currencies

h) Export credit guarantee insurance

i) Full responsibility for bad debt

j) Multi-currency and multi-language sales accounting.

Finding a factor

The Association of British Factors (ABF) provides a list of its members with a brief summary of services offered, regional offices and the approximate minimum client turnover. Alternatively, your bank manager will be able to advise you on a suitable local company, although since most banks now offer a factoring service it is likely they will offer their own services. Local companies are listed in the *Yellow Pages* under 'Factoring'.

Fees

A factoring company is paid for the service it provides in two ways, through interest payable on any sum advanced and through fees for specific services.

Interest is typically 3% over the bank base rate. The fees vary with the level of service provided. They range from 0.2% to 1% of invoice value for invoice discounting and from 2% to 3% for non-recourse factoring. The factor may submit two types of charge to his clients:

Discount charge

This charge is a discount on the purchase price of the debts (eg a deduction from the full face value of an invoice) – the factor does not pay the client the full value. The charge is usually comparable with overdraft rates.

Administration charge

The administration charge covers the cost of debt collection and sales ledger administration. It will usually be between 2.5% and 3.5% of the total debts collected.

Advantages of full-service factoring

i) Improves cash flow – invoices are settled in an average of 58 days (the ABF average) which is 15 days faster than the average for individual companies.

ii) Helps small companies without the required credit to raise large amounts of finance from banks.

iii) Provides funds in proportion to sales. The amount of finance available becomes greater as the business grows, so it is particularly helpful for businesses which are growing quickly.

iv) Allows management to focus more on business operations instead of finance administration.

v) Improves overall administration in terms of fewer and/or more effective staff.

vi) Provides access to expert financial services.

vii) Improves debt collection.

viii) Performs credit checks on existing and potential customers.

ix) Provides bad debt insurance.

x) Provides adequate access to working capital for some companies which have difficulty raising capital elsewhere and which could not otherwise stay in business.

Advantages for exporters

i) Allows a business to offer potential customers in overseas markets the same terms and conditions as local competitors.

ii) Makes business transactions with a foreign trade partner smoother by using the services of an expert in the local market.

iii) Offers protection against political and foreign exchange risk.

Disadvantages of factoring

i) Factoring is an expensive form of finance – it does nothing to help the balance sheet, only the cash flow.

ii) The business can lose full control of its sales ledger.

iii) The business has reduced contact with its customers, possibly hindering the development of long-term trade relations.

USEFUL TIPS

● *Consider factoring as a source of additional finance.*

● *Weigh up all of the options carefully.*

16 Minimising late payment problems

Introduction

All too often the problem of late payment is just accepted as a fact of life. As long as measures are being taken to chase and pursue debtors, managers feel comfortable that they are doing all they can to protect their cash flow. This can be a waste of resources and will frequently damage relations with clients who may still represent good sales potential, despite the payment problems.

It is important to understand how to control credit and recover debts, but it is far better to take measures to avoid the problem in the first place. Plans for legislation to combat late payment problems are currently under consideration at both UK and European levels; however businesses need to understand the individual needs of their customers in terms of invoicing and finance. Payment arrangements should be seen as part of the whole package of services the business offers its customers.

Trade credit

When a customer is allowed a period of time to pay for goods or services after they have been delivered, this is usually known as trade credit. Trade credit is not to be confused with consumer credit, which concerns offering special credit facilities to the general public and is not covered here. Most industrial markets have a customary period before payment is made (usually around 30 days). This varies according to the type of business concerned.

Credit is allowed for a number of reasons. Some businesses see it as a benefit to the customer and therefore a means to increase sales. Big businesses often demand credit because they have so much purchasing power. Often it is simply a convention of the trade that everyone follows.

Such conventions should not be accepted on a routine basis. If possible, credit limits should be set for each individual customer and reviewed regularly. Ideally, businesses should try to work on a cash on delivery basis. This can make sales more difficult, but at least the business knows where it stands financially. For many businesses, a significant proportion of company financial assets is tied up in late payments.

Late payment is recognised as a problem in the economy as a whole, a vicious circle where everyone is trying to delay payment as long as possible in order to retain cash in their business. For the individual business it is also a problem that can quickly get out of hand if it is not tightly controlled.

The customised approach

It is a mistake to see credit control as a routine accounting function with standardised credit limits and set procedures to pursue debtors. Payment arrangements should be seen as one dimension of your complete customer service. Responsibility to maintain customer satisfaction lies with every person in the company.

Customer care

Be proactive about customer relations. Contact the customer before there is a problem. Have they received the goods? Is everything in order? Have they received the invoice? Has it been correctly made out? If everything is in order payment should follow naturally. The customer knows about you, sees you as an ally, and hopefully will look forward to dealing with you again. If you only talk to them when there is a problem, customer relations can only deteriorate. Contact with the client should be controlled and consistent. Ideally, the person who agreed the initial deal should continue to be the main channel of communication to the customer, and all staff should have a consistent approach to customer care.

Quality awareness

Many companies today find themselves in difficulties when a major customer refuses to pay on the grounds that an order does not meet the required specification. Fewer problems will arise in companies which use quality management techniques. More specifically, it is important that you can exactly define the quality that the customer expects if they are not to find fault with what you deliver. Make sure this is defined in every detail and you have it in writing from the customer. Do not undertake a job which demands a level of quality that you cannot realistically achieve.

Maintain the cash flow cycle

The overall aim should be to maintain the flow of the cycle of payment, especially at critical points such as delivery and invoicing. If you only call up your debtors you are spending time dealing with people who have already shown that they are reluctant to pay. You can only expect limited returns from such activity.

Agreements in writing

Ensure that, once you have agreed a deal with a customer, you confirm it in writing. Obviously, if there is a legal dispute it is important to have evidence about the agreement or sale. On a more basic level though, it is surprising how often two people will come away from the same meeting with totally different ideas of what was agreed. The majority of late payments derive from an unanswered customer question. Misunderstandings, even if they are not serious, can delay payment. Try to ensure that all the details of any agreement are summarised in a document. This will reduce the chances of a dispute arising and help you resolve it if it does.

Customising payment arrangements

Agree payment methods that best suit the client:

i)   Credit limits should be agreed if possible for each client, and the terms should be reviewed on a regular basis.

ii) Can you offer a discount for prompt payments, especially discounts for cash? Such terms are usually only made available to those placing particularly large orders.

iii) Conversely, be prepared to charge interest for late payment. Such penalties should be written into a clause in the contract. However, recent moves towards legislating for statutory interest on late payments have been met with concern over the damage that this might do to customer relations. Collecting interest is often even harder than collecting the original sum and can ultimately lead to costly legal action.

iv) Try to establish from the outset whether the customer is likely to have any difficulties making the payment, particularly for large sums. Can payment be arranged in installments?

v) Asking for a deposit is a good test of the commitment of a customer and it establishes that they can pay.

Invoicing

Invoicing may seem straightforward, but a basic mistake can cause a major cash flow problem.

i) Invoice in the way that suits the customer, not your own administration. If the customer prefers invoicing in batches of a dozen rather than units, do it their way. If they have to change their system to suit your invoice, payment could be delayed.

ii) Invoice immediately. If you delay, how can you expect the customer to pay promptly?

iii) Invoice correctly. The place to invoice may not be at the point of delivery. It may even be an entirely different company. Double check that all the details are correct (and legible) before you send the invoice out.

iv) Single item invoicing. Payment for large quantities of items can be held up if the customer finds defects in only one part of the batch. One way to reduce this risk is to invoice for items singly or in smaller batches. This way payment will be delayed only for that part of the batch which is defective.

USEFUL TIPS

● *A senior member of staff should review the overdue debtors list on at least a monthly basis.*

● *Although it is important to maintain customer goodwill, you should try to become adept at spotting potential bad debtors. A large amount of credit information and advice is available to assist you in this process.*

- *Do not take late payment problems for granted. Look for the underlying reasons, inside and outside the company, and try to address them directly.*

- *Ensure that you have a way to obtain proof of delivery of all items in good order, and that delivery is to the correct destination. Disputes about delivery delay payment.*

17 Debt recovery

This section looks at how to get payment from those people who owe you money. It gives a general review of debt recovery and will not be sufficiently detailed for a particular case.

Introduction

Businesses need to know how to vet clients, help them pay on time, identify those who are not paying, and convert as many of these as possible into cash payers. Every effort should be made to ensure that the problem does not arise in the first place. Obtain specific advice on prevention and what to do when things go wrong from professional advisers.

Agreements with the customer

It is essential that once you have gained a customer, you tie them in legally. An oral agreement is sufficient to be a legally binding contract providing that the essential elements are included (ie offer, acceptance and consideration). It is, however, advisable to get a contract in writing to define the terms and conditions and prevent any later problems over evidence. Many firms have a standard statement of terms and conditions which they issue with written agreements. If the deal with the customer is clearly set down in writing, it is the basis to resolve any subsequent disputes as quickly as possible. It does not necessarily mean that you will immediately take them to court, but it will help if you need to do so.

Client vetting

After you allow credit to a customer they might go out of business, leaving you with a bad debt. Always try to research the security of a potential customer's trading position, particularly if a large amount of money is at stake. Many perfectly viable businesses are simply bad payers, so see if you can find out about their track record.

- **Get information from the customer**. A standard form is a good way to ensure that sufficient information is always obtained about the customer. Ask for:

   a) Name and address of the customer's bank and when the account was first opened. If the business claims to be well established and has a fairly new bank account, be suspicious. They could have opened it up under a false name and address. If an account is under two years old ask for details of the previous account.

b)   The customer's home address if it differs from the business address.

c)   In the case of limited companies, the registration number and date of incorporation.

d)   Names and addresses of any partners in a partnership.

e)   Name and address of at least one other firm presently supplying the customer on credit, and permission to approach them for a reference.

- **Take up the references**.

- **Get a credit rating**. A number of agencies compile records of the credit worthiness of companies. A rating may cost as much as £40, but it could well be worth it if you hope to do a lot of business with the client.

Handling late payment

You must have a systematic way to identify and pursue customers who fail to pay on time. This will very much depend upon the efficiency of your accounting systems and on how disciplined you are at keeping them up to date. For most small businesses, chasing debts will be a weekly activity, done in conjunction with the other accounting procedures.

It is important to work in a disciplined manner – customers should realise that they are expected to keep to the agreed terms, and that you will take decisive action if they do not. This can be difficult, but you should realise that it is an important and effective way to maintain your cash flow, and well worth doing. Research shows that frequent chasing results in quicker payment.

Equally, businesses have to balance the way they pursue their debtors with good customer relations. Such decisions vary according to the market. You do not want to jeopardise a good client relationship by being too heavy handed, especially if there has been a simple misunderstanding. On the other hand, some trades expect payment to be a cat and mouse affair.

The process has to be managed. It should not be done by rota. You must prioritise and take decisions. Which debtors are likely to pay up, and how much time can you afford to allocate to pursuing them? What will be the most effective way to put pressure on them? Who has an aptitude for this kind of work? Do they need training? How will you measure the effectiveness of your debt collecting process? Should you contract it out?

Written reminders and reissue invoices

Many businesses send out a reminder letter with a second copy of the original invoice. This procedure is only advisable if you deal with a large volume where some level of default is expected. Normally a small business should not automatically issue reminder letters: it can be an expensive waste of time and an excuse for your own delay. If you do issue written reminders, be very direct. Don't be apologetic, your customer has broken an agreement and you can afford to be quite forceful.

Chasing debts by telephone

Most small businesses have a more familiar relationship with their clients, so it may be more appropriate to contact the client direct to find out if there has been some kind of problem. Don't be afraid to use the telephone. A direct appeal can often get you further than a letter, and gives you the opportunity to find out more about the nature of the reason for non-payment. When making a call have all of the details of the invoice in front of you and speak to someone who can actually issue payment, eg the accounts clerk. Be brief and polite – offending the accounts clerk won't get you very far.

Factoring

Factoring companies buy unpaid invoices from their clients as they arise. This can release cash into the business quickly and allows it to concentrate solely on increasing sales. Factoring does not suit all businesses and should be used with great caution.

Debt recovery

When the debtor has been given a reasonable amount of time to pay, a decision about further action has to be made.

At this stage you are definitely in dispute with the client. It is a form of conflict and you have to know how to deal with it. Do not go in with all guns blazing; this may entrench the debtor more firmly. Apply increasing pressure gradually (but firmly) and always give the debtor opportunities to pay up without losing face. Stay calm at all times and reserve more serious measures for use at the most opportune time. Aim for a 'win – win' solution where both sides get a satisfactory outcome. An extended dispute, especially legal, can be expensive.

i)   Further telephone calls will be necessary. At this stage, the person that made the sale or closed the contract should be involved. If the matter cannot be cleared up over the telephone, arrange to meet with the client for a more in-depth discussion.

ii) Negotiated solutions. If the debtor is in financial difficulties, is there an alternative solution? Could the customer do some work for you free of charge? Can they give you some of their stock at cost price which you could sell on at a profit? Such solutions can sometimes be more productive than pursuing debtors through the courts.

iii) If the person is evasive and never available, you have to take things a stage further. Try collecting the debt yourself through a personal visit. Although you are forbidden by law to harass or threaten a debtor you may still visit their home.

iv) Sell the debt to a debt collection agency. These can be found in the *Yellow Pages*. You either sell a debt to them or they get a large commission on the debt once they have recovered it. This all depends on whether they feel they can recover it; you will probably receive only about 25-30% of the amount due.

Legal action

Taking legal action should be done with care, but is often much more straightforward than many expect. Whatever you do, it is advisable to consult a solicitor. They can advise you on whether the claim is worth pursuing, help you settle out of court, and if necessary, represent your interests in court. Many also have debt collecting and client vetting services.

i)   Solicitor's letter. A letter from a solicitor to a debtor can be very effective. Your solicitor may do this free or for a small charge.

ii) Statutory Demand for Payment. If the debt is over £750 and your demands for payment have been ignored you can send your debtor a 'Statutory Demand for Payment'. This is in fact a way of warning the debtor that you believe them to be insolvent/bankrupt, but it can be a very effective way to collect debts from perfectly viable businesses. None the less, it is quite an extreme action and should be done with care. The forms for such demands are available from legal stationers.

iii) Recover the debt through the courts. In straightforward and undisputed cases you can now seek to recover trade debts of any amount through the County Court without the use of a solicitor. If the debt is below

£3,000 you can use the Small Claims procedure. If the claim is disputed you will need to employ a solicitor.

iv) If the debtor is insolvent you may choose to take steps to enforce liquidation or bankruptcy so that you can make a claim on any remaining assets. Whether or not you do so will depend upon the size of the debt and on how many other debtors have a claim on the assets. If creditors are more likely to get their money that way, they might agree to a Voluntary Arrangement (VA), allowing the debtor to continue trading and gradually pay the debts off.

USEFUL TIPS

- *If you are dealing with a limited company which you think may be in financial trouble, try to obtain a personal cheque from a director. Such companies frequently have no assets and therefore are not worth suing.*

- *Be strict about credit terms when dealing with foreign firms as any legal action will be much more complicated.*

● *If a customer is reluctant to pay up immediately, then obtain a post dated cheque. Should it bounce, you can proceed quickly in the court and judgement is obtainable by a procedure that avoids the delays and costs involved if you sue on the contract.*

Investing
in a business

18 Valuing a business

This section looks at ways of calculating a value for a business which is not quoted on the Stock Exchange. The methods can be used by people buying into a business or by those selling all of, or their share in, a private limited company.

Introduction

Valuing an unquoted company is very difficult, yet can become important if either you are a business person seeking an external investor or you are an investor looking for an opportunity in which to invest. Ultimately, what a business is worth comes down to what both parties agree it is worth. Business owners, having decided to seek an external injection of equity, will be wanting to maximise the share capital provided whilst minimising the proportion of total shares given in exchange. Investors will be wanting to maximise their return on capital – usually defined as internal rate of return.

There are effectively three methods of valuing a business. Each of these is reviewed in turn overleaf.

Net asset method

This is the way of valuing a business that people understand most readily. The net assets figure, equal to the net worth, is shown on the balance sheet. If everything was sold at the value recorded on the balance sheet, the amount of money realised would be equal to the net assets. Sometimes buyers are reluctant to pay much more than net asset value, perhaps with a small premium in recognition of goodwill. This might typically be the case where a business, for example, is only making low profits.

The net assets figure may need to be adjusted to reflect the true worth of the assets. Buildings, for example, may be worth more than shown on the balance sheet. Equipment, especially computers, may be worth far less. Negotiations may be required about how assets will be valued, but take into account replacement value and realisable value.

As with using multiples of earnings (see opposite), it is very difficult to make a suitable allowance for goodwill. Often, one year's profit after tax is used.

Multiple of earnings

If you follow the business pages in the newspapers, you will be familiar with price/earnings
(p/e) ratios. This is the ratio of the price of one
share to the earnings (that is, the net profit after
tax) attributable to that share. The p/e ratio is one
of the figures provided on the share price page
for companies quoted on the Stock Exchange.
The price of shares varies depending (amongst
a number of factors) on the market's expectation
of future earnings. Some newspapers, such as
the *FT*, also quote average p/e ratios for each
business sector.

For example, for one day in December 1996,
the *FT* was quoting sector p/e ratios as follows:

Consumer goods (828 companies in sector)	17
Household goods (15)	14
Pharmaceuticals (14)	21
Services (252)	22
Media (44)	28
FTSE All share (895)	17
FTSE 100	16

The p/e ratio gives an indication of how much
investors are prepared to pay to buy the shares.
If, for example, Sage Group plc has earnings per

share (EPS) of 18.5p and one share costs around £5 then it has a p/e ratio of 27 (ie 500 divided by 18.5). You can apply this to any business. Take the net profit, apply a suitable multiplier and that gives the value of the business. You can make a first stab at selecting a suitable multiplier by looking at the p/e ratios for quoted companies, but you will need to apply a discount to take account of your smaller size, the greater risk and the difficulty for investors wishing to sell shares in private limited companies. Typically you should expect to apply a discount of 30-40 per cent, though if your profit is less than £1m, the discount should probably be at least 50 per cent, and possibly higher still.

For example, you have achieved annual earnings of £100,000 per annum over a number of years and can demonstrate that this is likely to continue into the future. In your business sector the average p/e ratio is 12 but you apply a discount of 50% to give a multiplier of 6. This implies that the business is worth £600,000. You should exclude non-recurring expenditure when calculating the earnings for a particular year.

Standard formulae

Standard methods of valuation have arisen in some sectors. These sometimes relate to measures other than financial measures though ultimately every measure is translatable into financial measures. For exampl, the cost of a milk round depends on the average daily delivery. Insurance brokers often use one to two times gross commission. It may be worth finding out if a formula is applied in the sector in which you are operating before committing yourself.

Dividing the shares

Valuing the business only gives you a starting point. If you are looking for an external investor, you then have to negotiate the proportion of shares that might be offered for a given amount of finance. The proprietors will have invested their own finance – though this should, in effect, be reflected in the valuation. They will also have invested considerable time and effort to build up the business to the point where they are seeking additional equity. This, too, should be recognised and rewarded. One way of doing this is to add a notional amount to the net asset valuation to represent the 'sweat equity' – that is, the hard work and effort you have already applied to build the business up to its current position but which is not reflected in the valuation of the business. If, for example, a business has a net asset valuation of £50,000, a further £50,000 might be added as sweat equity. An investor providing an additional £50,000 would then receive 33% of the shares.

USEFUL TIPS

- *You are aiming for an achievable valuation – one on which both parties can agree – so you need to be realistic. If using the price/earnings ratio method, select a realistic p/e ratio and discount it by an amount which is appropriate for the size of your business.*

- *Ideally, seek professional advice in valuing your business. If you are hoping to attract external equity, negotiate an allowance for your 'sweat equity'.*

19 Seeking venture capital

This section explains the process of seeking venture capital finance for the small to medium sized business.

Introduction

Venture capital is a means of financing a growing business whereby a portion of the share capital or equity is sold in return for a major investment in the business. Venture capital is usually attracted by businesses demonstrating the prospect of rapid growth often through some kind of product innovation.

For most small to medium sized businesses such funding goes hand in hand with changes of a fundamental nature. The company often must be restructured legally and new expertise brought in. The potential rewards are great, but owner managers in particular must be prepared to make the sacrifices that go with reporting to outside investors and delegating to a larger management team.

PART SEVEN · SECTION NINETEEN   **181**

Pros and cons

Pros

- No interest payments to make.

- Possibility of new contacts and management help.

- Can lever more debt finance if required.

- Focuses the business objectives and provides business structure and discipline.

- Strengthening of balance sheet and reduced gearing.

Cons

- Investors usually looking for a high return, often 35% plus.

- Can cost a lot in professional fees to professional advisers to comply with the Financial Services Act 1986.

- Requires giving up a stake in the business.

- May introduce short term thinking into the business.

- High demands on information.

- Owners must be prepared to share control and rewards.

Sources of venture capital

Venture capital funds come in a wide variety. Some specialise in particular industries. Some will consider start up propositions, or innovative products at an early stage in their development. Others finance the expansion of rapidly growing businesses or management buy-outs. It is important to target the right source for your own requirements.

Private investors

Private individuals have backed some of the most successful businesses in the UK. They can often be found via:

a) Professional advisers, accountants, solicitors, stockbrokers, bankers etc.

b) The Local Investment Networking Company (LINC) which helps small businesses find suitable private investors.

c) *Venture Capital Report* which is a monthly magazine detailing investment opportunities to mostly wealthy individuals.

d) Venture Capital Trusts (VCT) which encourage investment in unquoted companies by allowing the investor to claim tax relief on the investment.

e) Most banks which now have what are commonly known as 'business angels'.

This is where the bank maintains a network of individuals with the interest and financial backing to invest in businesses. Each bank's requirements are different so you will need to shop around.

Corporate investors

Often suppliers or purchasers invest in small companies as a way of expanding their interests. Key profiles are of companies with a good profitable core business but little room for market share increase.

Professional venture capitalists

These funders are usually highly selective about companies they invest in and tend to look at investing over £250,000 in a small portfolio of companies. Such companies range from small independent consultants to wholly owned subsidiaries of banks or pension funds and are likely to manage a portfolio of several funds.

Economic/social development funds

There are now a number of funds in the UK which invest in projects of a specified nature, area or industry. These include British Coal Enterprise and British Steel Industries (for business development in coal and steel closure areas). These funds will often support ventures that other funds will not even consider, especially if the manager(s) has no real track record.

Whatever route you take, the funding source will frequently operate through an intermediary, normally an experienced venture capital company. This allows the investor to benefit from the experience of the venture capitalist in making the investment decision. The venture capital company may also represent the investor on the board and/or provide financial and management consultancy support to the business.

What is the venture capitalist looking for?

This list provides a simple overview:

i)   Return on investment – usually at least 35% compounded annual capital growth.

ii) People with vision, self-confidence, drive and energy with aspirations to grow the business.

iii) Real marketing skills linked to management skills with leadership attributes.

iv) Market knowledge or a growing market and /or innovative product.

v)   An exit route, ie a chance to sell out within five to seven years either to the business itself, through a trade sale or by a flotation.

The process

Presenting the case

A clear and comprehensive plan needs to be presented. This needs to sell the idea and the strategy. The plan will include:

a)   Summary

b)   Background and business

c)   Past performance

d)   Market analysis

e)   Products

f)   Strategy for growth

g)   Operational aspects

h)   Management and organisation

i)   Financial projections and targets

j)   Capital requirements.

Preparation is likely to be a long drawn out affair requiring a lot of effort. It may be useful to produce a two page summary to test interest. If you get a meeting you are doing well, if they come and see you, even better. Remember that only one in twenty proposals are supported.

Investigation

If the proposal is of interest, the venture capitalist is likely to commission a more in-depth investigation upon which to base a final decision. The investor may commission a consultant to carry out an independent study. The venture capitalists will start taking a close interest in the business. There will be frequent visits and the investor will expect you to be completely candid about your business affairs. This is also a testing of relations from both points of view. Equity investments are frequently a partnership where mutual trust and respect is essential.

Negotiating the investment

Should the investigations prove fruitful, the investor will aim to close the deal as a written legal agreement. This will extend into changes that might be necessary in terms of the company structure. This is clearly a critical phase where good professional support is essential.

Monitoring performance

It is absolutely essential that you can provide regular up to date information to the investor. This will include monthly management accounts, minutes of board meetings, notification of major management decisions etc.

Professional support

Fund raising via a share issue is governed by detailed regulations and professional advice will always be required. Some investments will be governed by the Companies Act 1985 and the Financial Services Act 1986. Usually you will require the advice of a solicitor and an accountant.

Solicitors

A solicitor can advise you on your position and rights when negotiating the legal agreement for the investment. You will also need legal advice to comply with the law if you have to change the legal status of your company.

Accountants

The various funding packages available can be complicated and independent financial advice may be necessary to evaluate the options. New accounting systems may need to be introduced to ensure the investor can monitor performance.

Business advisers

Many new businesses have used experienced business advisers to help them put a growth funding package together. Such advisers have contacts in a variety of funding organisations which allows them to help the small business to negotiate an interdependent funding package comprising grants and loans as well as equity. Such support will also give the investor added confidence.

USEFUL TIPS

- *Always explore other sources of finance (eg grants, loans, factoring etc) as well as seeking venture capital.*

- *Be realistic. The chances of obtaining venture capital are not favourable. Less than 5% are successful.*

- *Remember, the venture capitalist once on board could be a major help with international contacts and experience.*

- *Try to research each source before you approach them. Most funds specialise and have minimum and maximum investment levels.*

- *It is very difficult to succeed on a DIY basis. Select your professional adviser carefully.*

- *Raising capital takes time, effort and money. Be careful that your business is not affected by the strain on resources. Be prepared to develop products to at least the prototype stage.*

- *When seeking venture capital pay closer attention to your personal characteristics and experience than the product, market or financial criteria listed.*

- *Complement your weaknesses by hiring people who are stronger on particular dimensions than yourself.*

Other

part.
eight

20 Tax, National Insurance and VAT

This section gives information on tax and National Insurance rates, reflecting changes introduced in the Budget of March 1998.

Introduction

The payment of tax is a legal obligation. Businesses assist the government in collecting tax through the PAYE and VAT system. It is important to be able to manage the administration to allow for the impact of tax payments on your cash flow, and to take advantage of whatever tax breaks are available. Your accountant should be able to help you to achieve this. This section gives a brief overview of taxation together with details of the current rates of taxation.

Income tax

Income tax is payable by any individual who receives an annual income. This includes income derived from paid employment or from the profits of any trade, profession or vocation. Income tax is charged at different rates according to the amount earned. Personal and other allowances reduce the amount of income that may be taxed. Tax years run from 6 April to 5 April.

Sole traders and partnerships

Sole traders pay income tax on the profit which their business makes. In partnerships, the profit is divided between the partners as stated in the deed of partnership and then each is taxed as for sole traders.

Drawings

Sole traders and partnerships are taxed on the whole profit which the business makes, ie before 'drawings'. Drawings is the term used for money taken out of the profits for sole traders/partners to live on. The remaining profits are reinvested in the business. Income tax is charged on the whole amount – not just on the drawings which the owners choose to take out.

Revenue expenditure and capital allowances

Business expenditure is divided into revenue expenditure and capital expenditure. Revenue expenditure such as materials, overheads, wages for employees and allowable business expenses are deducted from income in order to arrive at net profit.

Capital expenditure covers assets such as cars, office equipment, machinery, etc. To account for the need to renew these assets periodically, businesses deduct 'depreciation' from their profits. Depreciation is not allowable as a deduction against taxable profits since you set your own level of depreciation. Instead capital expenditure is allowed for by a 'capital allowance'. Where a business spends £100,000 or more in a year on assets with working lives of 25 years or more, special rules apply. Small and medium sized businesses which invest in plant or machinery before 1 July 1998 will qualify for a capital allowance of 50% in the first year. After 1 July 1998, the first year allowance will become 40%. In both cases, subsequent years, an allowance of 25% of the reducing balance may be claimed. An accountant should be able to help you make best use of allowances.

When revenue expenditure and capital allowances have been deducted from your income, the remainder is profit. The sole trader's personal allowance (including 50% of Class 4 NI contributions) is deducted from the profit and the remainder is subject to income tax at the current rate.

Current year basis of assessment

For most sole traders or partnerships the payment of income tax works as follows:

Tax is assessed on the profit of the accounting year that ends in the tax year itself, rather than in the previous tax year as used to be the case. For example, the business makes up its accounts for the trading year ending 30 April 1998. The accounts must be submitted by a deadline in October 1998. Tax is assessed under the rates for 1998/9, with payments due on 31 January and 31 July 1999.

Self assessment

The 1994 Finance Bill aimed to simplify the system for taxing the self-employed. In particular it introduced the option of self-assessment. There are major implications for small businesses, and you are advised to seek help from an accountant.

Employees

Under the Pay As You Earn (PAYE) scheme, the employer deducts income tax and National Insurance from their employee's earnings and makes the payments to the government. Firms with an average combined bill for PAYE and NI contributions not exceeding £600 per month may make payments quarterly.

Corporation tax

If the business is registered as a company, then it is liable to pay corporation tax (CT). Again, tax is only levied on the profits which the business makes. The principals of the company pay income tax on their salaries as with any other employee.

There is a standard rate (31% reducing to 30% from April 1999) of Corporation Tax where profits exceed £1,500,000. Up to £300,000, the company pays tax at the Small Companies Rate (21% reducing to 20% from April 1999). Those with profits between £300,000 and £1,500,000 are taxed at the Small Companies Rate for the amount up to £300,000, with marginal relief where profits are between £300,000 and £1,500,000.

National Insurance rates

There will be major changes to the NI system from April 1999. At present, there are three applicable classes of National Insurance.

Class 1 Contributions

Class 1 National Insurance contributions apply to employed people and are paid by both the employer and the employee. It is the responsibility of the employer to pay both contributions, deducting the employee's contributions through the PAYE scheme.

No tax or NI is payable for any employee earning up to £64 per week. Employees do not pay contributions on earnings over £485 a week. Contracted out rates on earnings between £64 and £485 are reduced by 1.6% for employees and 3% for employers.

A rebate of up to the first year's NI contributions is to be available for businesses which take on someone who has previously been unemployed for two years or more.

Class 2 Contributions

Class 2 National Insurance is a flat rate (£6.35 pw for 1998/9)paid by all self-employed people, whether sole traders or partners.

If earnings are below £3,590 per year, there may be an entitlement to a refund, though this may affect entitlement to benefits. (See leaflet N127A available from Social Security Offices).

Class 4 Contributions

Class 4 NI contributions are payable by the self-employed, at the rate of 6% of assessable profits between £7,310 and £25,220.

Value Added Tax (VAT)

This is tax paid on the value added at each stage of delivery of a product or service. Not all goods are taxable – for example, some education and training, and postal services are exempt. If items are taxable there are three rates:

- Standard (17.5%)

- Zero Rated (0%)

- Zero rated items are different from exempt items.

VAT payments are normally made each quarter to the Customs and Excise. It is only necessary to register if business sales are taxable. You must register for VAT if your turnover is over £50,000. It may, however, be advantageous to register voluntarily if sales are below the turnover limit, because the VAT paid on purchases can be reclaimed. It is also possible to reclaim VAT on capital equipment, raw materials, and stocks bought before registration, provided the business still owns them. Businesses with a turnover of less than £300,000 can submit one annual return, otherwise returns must be submitted quarterly. If you are VAT registered you need tax invoices showing your VAT number, an analysed VAT account, and VAT return forms.

Company car and fuel benefits

Employees who have a car bought for them by their employer are taxed on the benefit which this provides to them. This is achieved by an adjustment to the tax code which effectively adds an amount to the employee's salary, thus increasing the amount of income tax which they must pay. This amount, the taxable benefit, is 35% of the original list price of the car including accessories. This is reduced by one third if the car is over four years old. If the mileage is 2,500 or over per annum, the benefit is reduced by one third, and by two thirds if the mileage is 18,000 or over.

Similarly, of fuel bought by the employer for private use is treated as a taxable benefit.

Both businesses and employees may benefit from doing away with company cars – opting instead for employees using their own vehicles and being reimbursed for business mileage.

21 Choosing and using an accountant

This section outlines the core services an accountant can offer and suggests ways of finding a suitable company.

Introduction

Most people think of accountants as being fully trained and qualified in their field, belonging to a professional body which regulates their work and being up to date with current legislation. When looking for an accountant for the first time you may want to ensure that they measure up.

Anyone can call themselves an accountant or a book keeper and provide a service to keep the books of a business in order. Such people vary widely in their ability to advise businesses on their operations from a financial point of view. Those with the most training, and offering the widest range of services, are likely to be members of one of the main professional accounting bodies. In the UK these are the Institutes of Chartered Accountants for England and Wales, Scotland, and Ireland, the Chartered Association of Certified Accountants (ACCA), and the Chartered Institute of Management

Accountants (CIMA). All of these bodies require those accountants who prepare or audit accounts in return for fees to hold the necessary practising certificate. These are renewed yearly if the accountant complies with the body's requirements on professional indemnity insurance, continuing professional development and continuity of practice arrangements.

Services offered by an accountant

An accountant can provide advice on and assistance with such issues as:

i) Whether it is necessary to register for VAT or PAYE, and the procedures involved.

ii) The tax implications of working from home.

iii) The tax implications of employing family members.

iv) What type of accounting system is needed.

v) Keeping proper books of account to meet relevant legal requirements. Many firms use accountants or book-keepers to prepare their accounts for them, although there is a danger that managers of small firms can lose touch with up-to-date financial information if they pass on all of the responsibility.

If you have set up in business as a partnership the rights and responsibilities of each partner should be defined in the partnership deed. An accountant can advise on issues relevant to partnerships, including:

i)   The amount of capital to be introduced.

ii) Division of profits.

iii) Calculation of individual tax liabilities.

iv) Adjustments necessary when a partner leaves or joins the firm.

There are more government regulations covering the activities of limited companies (contained in the various Companies Acts, etc) and these add considerably to the time and money spent on administration. This includes:

i)   The preparation of annual accounts including profit and loss account, balance sheet, source and application of funds flow statement.

ii) Limited companies with annual turnovers exceeding a limit (currently £350,000) are subject to an annual audit, whereby an independent accountant (who must be a registered auditor) examines the books and records to ensure that the company accounts represent a 'true and fair' view of the company's financial position.

Using an accountant

An accountant may be used to assist you in any of the following areas:

Legal requirements

a) Every business registered for VAT must keep records which satisfy the requirements of Customs and Excise.

b) The Inland Revenue requires every business to keep proper books of account for tax purposes (including for Self Assessment). Sole traders must file Self Assessment Tax Returns.

c) The Inland Revenue requires every business employing staff, no matter what its structure, to keep proper records for PAYE and the calculation of tax liabilities.

d) The Companies Act requires that every company keep proper records of money received and paid, of all sales and purchases, and of all assets and liabilities.

e) All limited companies are required by the Companies Act to file annual accounts laid out in a particular way and disclosing specified information.

f) The annual audit is another statutory requirement applying to many limited companies (see above).

Internal control

Knowledge of the costs of different functions and services is essential if your business is to grow stronger. Your accountant will be able to advise you on setting up the most effective form of management information system for your needs.

An efficient system will provide information for a number of areas including:

a) Information to help you get the pricing decision right. This requires a system for determining costs, selling prices and profit margins.

b) Good cash management is very important. Your accountant will be able to advise you on the preparation of such methods of financial control as forecast cash inflows and outflows, break-even analysis, business ratios and discounted cash flows. Accountants can be particularly helpful in developing budgets, comparing them with actual figures, identifying key variances and evaluating performance.

Raising finance

An accountant can advise on the best way for you to raise additional finance. They may suggest any of the following:

a) An overdraft is usually the best way to finance a temporary cash shortage.

b) For longer term cash flow problems a bank loan is usually the most suitable form of additional finance.

c) Factoring and invoice discounting, a house re-mortgage or a debenture loan are other forms of finance which could be considered.

Managing growth

An accountant can ensure your financial systems are effective and able to cope with company expansion. Adequate working capital, good controls over stock, invoicing, credit control and cash collection are among the most important aspects of good financial management in a growing business.

As a business expands, the volume of transactions, etc will inevitably increase. Your accountant may be able to assist in such tasks as payroll preparation, additional book-keeping, etc.

Buying a business

One way to set up in business is to take over an existing business as a going concern. In such a situation an accountant's advice will be invaluable; it is difficult to estimate how much a business is worth as there is rarely a market comparison available. The calculation of goodwill is particularly important.

An accountant's advice will also be needed in such situations as disposal of a business, mergers and management buy-outs.

Minimising business tax

Taxation can be a very large business expense. An accountant will be able to advise on such issues as the dates chosen to start and end the business year (which may affect your tax position); expenses which are tax deductible; the tax implications of purchasing or leasing capital equipment. Your accountant can also help you to prepare your tax return. There are different tax requirements for companies and sole traders. Corporation tax only applies to limited companies, sole traders are taxed under Income Tax rules.

Personal finances

a) **Personal Income Tax**. There are a number of ways to reduce income tax liability. Your accountant will be able to advise on such issues as choosing a form of borrowing/investment to best suit your tax position. Independent taxation of husbands and wives is another issue to be considered.

b) **Capital Gains Tax and Inheritance Tax**. Your accountant will be able to advise on insurance protection against Inheritance Tax, tax-free gifts, business relief, the use of trusts and the preparation of capital transfer tax returns.

c) **Insurance and Retirement Planning**. Accident insurance, life assurance and a retirement pension are essential aspects of personal financial planning.

d) **Wills**. Accountants may be appointed as executors as the terms of a will often need professional advice, especially if large sums of money are involved.

Fees

You should get a good idea of how much an accountant's fees are going to be in the first meeting. However, it can be difficult to predict exactly how much time will have to be devoted to a client's affairs. The fee charged is usually based on an hourly rate. This rate will vary depending on the levels of skill and responsibility required by the accountant for the task.

Most firms will calculate how much to charge each client by recording how much time was spent by all the firm's employees and partners on the assignment for that client. Each employee will be 'charged out' based on their level of superiority in the firm and their range of experience, so more junior staff members will carry out the more basic tasks.

Finding an accountant

When choosing an accountant it is advisable to stick to members of major accountancy bodies (look for the initials ACA, FCA or ACCA after their names), as there is no legislation in place to prevent totally inexperienced people from setting up as accountants. Check that they have a current (and recognised) practising certificate. Personal recommendation is perhaps one of the best ways to choose an accountant. You could contact the accounting associations for lists of their members in your area. Alternatively, you could try your bank manager, or adverts in *Yellow Pages*. The type of practice best suited to you will depend on such factors as the size of the job, specialist skills involved (no accountant is expert in all aspects of finance) and of course, the fees. The majority of firms operating in public practice employ chartered or certified accountants. The ACCA publishes a topographical directory of practising firms which is available to members of the public free of charge on request.

A professional accountant should issue a letter of engagement which sets out what work the accountant will do and how much will be charged. This must be signed by both the accountant and the client.

● *Find yourself an accountant as soon as you decide to set up in business. Receiving advice from the start can prevent problems in the future.*

● *Shop around to find the firm best suited to your needs. Make sure that you are not expected to pay for any discussion time which is purely part of the selection process (but do not expect them to do any work for you without payment).*

● *Find out the basis on which fees are calculated before you choose your accountant.*

● *Agree with your accountant the level of services required – if you are not specific, your accountant may end up doing more or less than you expected.*

● *Don't wait to complain if the service you are receiving is not to your satisfaction.*

● *Don't be afraid to question and negotiate fees.*

Appendices

22 Glossary of finance terms

This section is a glossary of the terms associated with finance for small to medium sized businesses.

Accountant: Professional who prepares or audits the accounts of a business.

Accounting: Recording and analysis of data about financial transactions. Usually involves the use of recognised techniques, practices and assumptions.

Accounting Code: Code numbers or letters assigned to budget or cost centres within an organisation to simplify allocation of income and expenditure.

Accounts: Financial records of a business. May be presented for analysis in the Profit & Loss Account and the Balance Sheet.

Accruals: Under the concept of accruals, revenue and costs are recognised in the accounts for the period in which they are earned or incurred – which may not be the same period in which payment is received or made.

Accrued Expenses: Amounts relating to expenditure incurred in the current accounting period for which the invoice, etc has not been received until the next accounting period.

Acid Test Ratio: See *Quick Ratio*.

Added Value: The value that you add to a product or service. It depends more upon what the customer is willing to pay than on the intrinsic value of what you sell. See also Pricing.

Amortization: Writing off an asset (eg a lease) over a period. May be used to mean depreciation.

Appropriation Account: The part of the profit and loss account which explains how the profit has been divided or appropriated.

Assets: Goods, resources and property belonging to the business.

Audit: Detailed inspection of a firm's financial records to determine their accuracy. A legal requirement for most limited companies, audits must be signed and registered by an accountant who is a qualified auditor.

Authorised Capital: Maximum share capital a company is allowed to issue under its memorandum of association.

Bad Debts: Debts which cannot be recovered and must be written off.

Balance Sheet: Statement showing the assets and liabilities of a business at any particular moment.

Bankruptcy: Where an individual or a business is unable to pay creditors in full. Being in a state of insolvency.

Base Rate: UK interest rate set by government policy for banks, etc to follow. Most banks charge interest above base rate with the amount above the base representing the perceived risk of lending to that customer.

Book-keeping: Recording the financial transactions of a business in its books and keeping those accounts in order for review or VAT inspection. Many small firms can use a book-keeper (who need have no formal qualifications) instead of an accountant; others use both.

Book Value: Value of an asset as shown in the accounting records. Book value usually means original value less accumulated depreciation.

Books: The business' financial records – Cash Book, Sales Ledger, Purchase Ledger and Wages Book.

Break-even Point: Point at which income from sales exactly equals all the business' costs.

Budget: Plan for the allocation and use of resources, often involving production of an itemised list of expected income and expenditure for a given period.

Business Angel: Someone with money seeking a company to invest in in the hope of a high future return.

Business Plan: Detailed plan of future business activity used as a guide by the management and the basis for applications for funds from potential investors.

Capital: Finance supplied by the proprietors of a business in order to acquire the resources (assets) with which to operate.

Capital Employed: The net worth of the business (capital introduced plus retained profit) plus long-term loans. Some definitions miss out long-term loans, others add short-term loans.

Capital Gains Tax: Tax on the profits accrued from the sale of capital assets (eg premises) and capital interests (eg shares in other firms).

Cash: Money in hand or in a bank account.

Cash Book: This records all receipts and payments.

Cash Flow: The money coming into and going out of a business in a given period. Cash flow may be positive or negative.

Cash Flow Forecast: Projection of future cash flow to give an idea of business viability and the amount of working capital required. Business plans should include a cash flow forecast.

Collateral: Security for a loan, eg a third party guarantee or borrower's property.

Components: Stock items to be used in the manufacturing process.

Consolidated Accounts: The accounts of a parent/holding company which combine the accounts of subsidiary companies.

Consumer Credit: Provision of credit to end customers, eg through hire purchase or deferred payment. The Consumer Credit Act must be adhered to.

Contingent Liability: Liability which is dependent upon future events.

Contribution: Income generated by a sale less the direct cost of sale.

Corporation Tax: Tax on company profits.

Cost of Sales: Costs clearly attributable to production.

Costing: Identifying the costs associated with business activities and sharing them out on a proportional basis.

Credit: In double entry terms, a credit balance in your accounts reflects a liability because you owe money to your creditor. If you are 'in credit' with a supplier, it means either they are willing to provide you with goods and services (up to a credit limit) without prior payment (or payment on delivery) or that you have paid them money which they owe you either in cash or in kind.

Credit Limit: A limit on borrowing from a bank or supplier, or that you impose on your own customers.

Credit Note: Document given to a customer or received from a supplier to adjust for invoicing errors or return of faulty goods, which shows that they are in credit to a certain amount.

Credit Period: Time allowed between the provision of goods or services and when they have to be paid for.

Creditors: Those to whom money is owed for goods, cash, services, etc. Suppliers who are owed money are described as 'trade creditors' to differentiate them from others, eg the bank. They are usually shown separately on the balance sheet.

Creditors' Turnover Ratio: A measure of how regularly a firm pays its creditors.

Current Assets: Assets in a cash or near cash state (eg cash, debtors, stock).

Current Liabilities: Debts owed by a firm which have to be paid back within the next financial year.

Current Ratio: A financial ratio which measures the ratio of current assets to current liabilities. Indicates whether the firm has sufficient working capital.

Customs and Excise: Government agency which controls imports and exports and collects customs duty, excise duty and VAT.

Debenture Loan: A loan, usually secured upon business assets, to be repaid on an agreed date with periodic (usually annual or bi-monthly) interest payments.

Debit: A record in the accounts of a sum owed to you. An account with a negative balance is said to be in debit.

Debt: Money borrowed to finance the business, eg in the form of an overdraft or a debenture. Money owed to suppliers is also debt.

Debtors: Businesses or individuals who owe the business money.

Debtors' Turnover Ratio: A measure of how quickly a firm's debtors pay their debts. Calculated as sales divided by average debtors. Dividing 365 by the result gives the average debt collection period.

Deficit: Shortfall between money available and money required.

Depreciation: The fall in value of fixed assets over time. An allocation (division) of the cost of the fixed assets over their useful, or income generating, lives. Depreciation does not involve actual receipts or payments; it is a book entry charged to the profit and loss account.

Direct Costs: Sometimes known as Cost of Sales, the costs that can be directly attributed to the production of a particular product or service eg raw materials, direct labour.

Disbursement: Money paid out, especially as cash, for incidental expenses.

Discount: A deduction from the price of an item, or a bonus for prompt payment.

Discounted Cash Flow: Technique for comparing projects to see which may give the best return on investment. Used when two projects will bring income at different times, allowing that money now is worth more than money in the future.

Dividend: Payment made from profit after tax to the owners of a company.

Double Entry: Method of book-keeping where every transaction is entered as a debit to one account and a credit to another account. The totals of debits and credits should be equal.

Drawings: Self-employed persons will draw money from their business at regular intervals. Known as drawings, this is an advance against profit. You are taxed on the profit, not on drawings.

ECU: see European Currency Unit.

Equity: This is the (shareholders') capital introduced by the owners, together with any retained earnings.

Euro: Name of the proposed single currency of the European Union.

European Currency Unit (ECU): Official unit of account for transactions within the European Union.

Expenses: General term which can mean all the costs of a business, but normally used to signify overhead expenses (as opposed to direct costs).

Factoring: Handing a firm's debtor book to a third party agent who pays the firm a proportion of each debt when it falls due and any remainder, less a service charge, upon successful collection of the debt.

Finance House: A company whose business is lending money.

Financial Ratio: see Ratio Analysis.

Financial Services: Term covering banking, building societies, insurance, etc.

Financial Year: The 12 month period which a company chooses for its accounting year.

Finished Goods: Stocks of goods which are ready to sell.

Fixed Assets: Assets with a life of longer than one year, eg buildings, machinery, etc.

Fixed Costs: Costs which are fixed for the business for a reasonable length of time, and not dependent on the number of units produced, eg rent, rates, salaries, etc.

Gearing: A measure of debt as a proportion of total finance. The ratio of debt to debt plus equity.

Goodwill: An intangible asset of a business, made up of regular customers, reputation, etc. Usually taken into account if the business is sold.

Grants: Financial assistance given to a business by a third party (eg a local authority). Grants do not usually have to be repaid provided agreed terms are met.

Gross Profit: Normally the sales income less the direct costs. For many small businesses this will be the same as the contribution.

Gross Profit Margin: Gross profit divided by sales; usually expressed as a percentage.

Hire Purchase: Purchase method where the buyer pays a deposit then regular payments to cover cost plus interest. Until the final installment is paid the goods are the seller's legal property.

Historical Costing: Recording and analysing costs after they are incurred at the actual cost.

Income Tax: Tax on an individual's income.

Indirect Costs: Business costs that cannot be directly attributed to production of a particular product or service (eg bank charges).

Inheritance Tax: Tax payable by the new owner or the transferor on assets transfered upon the death of the previous owner. May also be payable on certain transfers during the transferor's lifetime and on the transferor's death in respect of other lifetime transfers.

Inland Revenue: Government agency responsible for collecting UK income taxes.

Input Tax: VAT that a taxable business pays on the stock, materials and capital goods that it buys, and on goods or services it uses. VAT paid on items for business use may be reclaimable.

Insolvency: When a person or business is unable to meet debts when they fall due.

Intangible Assets: Items, such as goodwill, included as assets on the balance sheet because they have a perceived value but which have no physical form.

Interest: Money paid to a lender in return for use of their loan finance.

Interest Cover: Measure of the ease with which a business can meet its interest payments. Calculated as profit before interest and tax divided by interest paid.

Invariable Costs: Costs which do not vary with the number of units produced.

Inventory: Stock items or a list detailing them. In accounting, inventory is the sum of raw materials, components, work in progress and finished goods.

Investment: Spending, eg to buy assets, in the hope of receiving income or a larger repayment in return. Return on investment is a measure of business performance.

Invoice: Document listing goods or services supplied and amounts due.

Invoice Discounting: Where a third party pays an advance on the value of an invoice which is not yet due for payment. Interest is deducted plus a service charge.

Lease Purchase: A variation on leasing. At the end of the lease period the goods become the leasee's property.

Leasing: Where the owner of property (eg premises, machinery) makes its use over to a business or individual for a specified period at an agreed rent.

Leverage: Ratio of total finance to equity (ie ratio of debt plus equity/equity). More commonly a US term; the UK term is gearing.

Liabilities: Combined debts owed by a firm.

Liquid Assets: Cash or items that can readily be converted into cash.

Liquidation: Formal closing down of a business. Any assets are sold and used to pay off some or all of the firm's debts.

Liquidity: Measure of the working capital or cash available to a business to enable it to meet its liabilities as they fall due. Liquidity ratios include the current ratio and the quick ratio (also known as the 'acid test').

Loans: Funds borrowed by a business, usually secured on a business asset, repaid over an agreed period with an agreed level of interest.

Loss: Where expenditure exceeds income in a given period.

Management Accounts: Detailed financial information provided with the needs of business managers in mind.

Management Buy In: Purchase of an existing business and its management by a new owner.

Management Buy Out: Purchase of all or part of an existing business by its existing managers.

Margin of Safety: Describes how far above break-even the business is operating. The greater the margin the less sensitive the business will be to falls in sales, etc.

Marginal Costing: The extra cost of producing one extra unit. Marginal costing compares the marginal revenue (the extra income) of selling the extra unit with the marginal cost.

Mark-up: Difference in the price of goods or services introduced by a supplier. A manufacturer might add a mark-up to the cost of manufacturing to provide a profit. A retailer may add a further mark-up to cover overheads and generate profit.

National Insurance (NI): Government operated scheme of insurance against ill health and unemployment. Partly funds the NHS, unemployment benefits, state pensions, etc. Both employers and employees contribute to the scheme.

Negative Cash Flow: Where more money is going out of the business than is coming in.

Net Current Assets: Current assets minus current liabilities. This should be positive, otherwise the business may not be able to meet debts as they fall due.

Net Finance: See Net Worth.

Net Present Value: An estimate of the present value of the expected future cash flows of a project.

Net Profit: See Operating Profit.

Net Profit Margin: Net profit divided by sales and expressed as a percentage.

Net Worth: The money introduced by the shareholders or owners together with retained earnings (reserves) less total liabilities.

Operating Profit: Actual profit made by the business after deduction of all expenses except interest. For self-employed persons, drawings are not regarded as an expense, however wages for company directors and staff are. Tax is not an expense.

Output Tax: VAT due on taxable goods or services supplied to a customer.

Overdraft: Where a withdrawal or payment made from a bank account takes out more than was in it. Banks may agree an overdraft limit (the maximum amount they will allow the customer to go overdrawn by) but will charge interest and may require additional fees. Often used as a short term business finance facility; but can be cancelled by the bank at any time.

Overhead Costs (Overheads): All operating costs which are not direct and which, generally speaking, are fixed costs.

Overtrading: When a business is selling more products or services than the working capital facilities can cope with.

PAYE (Pay As You Earn): All employers are required to deduct income tax from employees' pay. The system uses tax codes to adjust the level of deductions from each employee's pay.

Payroll: The list of a firm's employees who receive regular payments.

Personal Expenses: Expenses incurred by an individual whilst on company business; not normally reclaimable as business expenses.

Positive Cash Flow: Where more money is coming into the business than is going out of it.

Pricing: Goods and services can be priced by taking the cost of providing them and adding a mark-up for profit. Some firms add a fixed percentage. It can be more profitable to look at demand and what customers are willing to pay. Customers are paying for the added value that you give.

Prior Charge: Where the terms of a loan give the lender a priority claim on a firm's assets used as security should the firm go into liquidation.

Profit: Level by which income exceeds expenditure in a given period.

Profit and Loss Account: Summary of all income and expenditure for a defined accounting period.

Profit Margin: Ratio of profit to sales; calculated using either gross profit (gross profit margin) or profit before interest and tax (net profit margin). Often expressed as a percentage (100 x profit divided by sales).

Purchase Ledger: Used to record all suppliers' invoices and payments to suppliers and to show which are unpaid.

Qualified Accounts: Audited company accounts where the auditor has expressed doubts or disagreement over the information shown in the accounts.

Quick Ratio: A financial ratio which measures how readily a firm can pay off its debts. It is the ratio of cash and debtors to current liabilities. Also called acid test ratio.

Ratio Analysis: Reviewing a firm's performance by looking at the way particular figures in the accounts relate to each other. Four main types of ratio look at liquidity, solvency, efficiency and profitability. The Centre for Interfirm Comparison publishes average ratios for particular industries.

Raw Materials Stock: Stocks of materials held by a manufacturer for future use.

Receivership: Where a bankrupt firm's affairs are being administered by a court appointed official receiver.

Reducing Balance: Method of accounting for the depreciation of a fixed asset over its expected useful life.

Reserves: Profits retained within the business. Reserves show where the money came from, not how it has been used. It may exist as cash in the bank, but more likely will have also financed working capital (as shown in stock and work in progress).

Return on Investment: Amount of money generated in a given period of time for the investment of a given amount of capital.

Revenue: Income generated by the business for a specific period.

Revenue Account: Record of company income and expenditure which excludes capital income and expenditure.

Salary: Regular payments to an employee, especially office workers.

Sales Ledger: Record of every invoice issued, the amount of cash received and the amount due to the business.

Security: Guarantee given by a borrower to a lender. The lender may be given a prior charge over assets.

Self Assessment for Tax: The government has now made many individuals responsible for calculating their own tax liability and reporting the details to the Inland Revenue.

Shareholders: Owners of a company's shares or stocks.

Shares: The ownership of a company is divided into shares, each representing a part of the equity capital invested in the business.

Soft Loan: Loan made at a low interest rate or with lenient repayment terms.

Solvency: Measure of a business's ability to pay its bills as they fall due. If it cannot pay, then it is insolvent. A negative net worth indicates a business is insolvent.

Spreadsheet: Computer software useful for cash flow analysis, producing budgets, etc.

Staged Payments: Payment by installments. May be a normal condition in a contract or arranged as a way of improving cash flow where the customer cannot pay the full amount due in one payment.

Start-up Costs: Costs specifically associated with setting up in business.

Stock: Goods held for sale in the ordinary course of business. Raw materials, components and consumables may also be held in stock.

Stock Exchange: A centre where shares in public companies are traded.

Straight Line: Method of accounting for the depreciation of a fixed asset across its estimated useful life.

Tangible Assets: Real assets which belong to a firm, and are not intended for resale; eg premises, machinery, etc, but not stock or goodwill.

Tax Evasion: Illegal attempts to pay less tax, eg by forging expenses or hiding income.

Taxable Supplies: Goods and services supplied to a customer which are liable for VAT (even if zero rated).

Taxable Turnover: Total value of taxable supplies including VAT. Excludes any exempt goods and services.

Tax Planning (Avoidance): Reducing or deferring the amount of tax that needs to be paid by making best use of available allowances and claiming for all allowable expenses.

Trial Balance: In double entry book keeping, checking to see if all debit and credit items in a ledger have the same total.

Turnover: Total sales income. Net Turnover is total sales less returns, excluding VAT.

Value Added Tax (VAT): Tax on consumer spending which applies to the value added to a product at each stage of its production and distribution. VAT is collected in stages by VAT registered firms. The consumer pays the full amount of the tax but at each stage up to that point firms handling the goods pay input tax to their suppliers and collect output tax from their customers. The VAT that the firm pays to Customs & Excise = Output Tax minus Input Tax.

Variable Costs: Costs which vary with production levels, eg direct costs such as raw materials. However, other costs, such as power consumption, may also vary and these need to be taken into account.

VAT: see Value Added Tax.

VAT Registration: Businesses whose turnover in the past 12 months exceeds a threshold (or is expected to exceed it within the next 30 days) must register with Customs & Excise. The threshold is currently £50,000 of taxable supplies.

Venture Capital: Funding which may be made available to businesses with good prospects of growth. Venture capital providers often take a significant involvement in the business.

Wages: Regular payments to an employee, especially a manual worker.

Wages Book: Records wages and salary payments made to employees.

Winding Up: Voluntary or compulsory liquidation of a business.

Work in Progress: Raw materials, components and products which are within the production process but are not yet finished goods.

Working Capital: The difference between current assets and current liabilities. In practice, this figure will vary over the year so the minimum working capital requirement is the maximum difference that occurs during the period.

Write Off: To reduce the value of an asset in the books to zero (eg to record a debt as being a bad debt.)

Written Down Value: When the book value of an asset is reduced to take depreciation into account, the new value is the written down value.

Zero Based Forecasting: Forecasting which starts from a zero base rather than from the previous year's actual performance figures.

23 Further reading

Introduction

Built to Last: Successful Habits of Visionary Companies, John Collins and Jerry Porras, Harper Collins, 1994

Section 1

Financial Control for Non-Financial Managers, David Irwin, Pitman, 1995

Section 2

Financial Control for Non-Financial Managers, David Irwin, Pitman, 1995

Planning to Succeed in Business, David Irwin, Pitman, 1995

Section 3

Financial Control for Non-Financial Managers, David Irwin, Pitman, 1995

How To Maintain Positive Cash Flow, Gillian Clegg, Business Books Limited, 1991

Small Business Survival, Roger Bennett, Pitman Publishing, 1991

Section 4

Financial Control for Non-Financial Managers, David Irwin, Pitman, 1995

Pocket Accountant Notes, Nobes, The Economist Publications, 1985

Statement of Standard Accounting Practice No 12, Institute of Chartered Accountants

Section 5

Financial Control for Non-Financial Managers, David Irwin, Pitman, 1995

Understanding Company Accounts, B Rothenberg and J Newman, Kogan Page, 1993

Section 6

Financial Control for Non-Financial Managers, David Irwin, Pitman, 1995

Book-keeping and Accounts, Frank Wood, Pitman, 1992

Simple Cash Book for Small Businesses, Paul Ordidge, Kogan Page, 1989

Basic Book-keeping and Accounts, Beryl Wilkinson, Stanley Thornes, 1990

Section 7

Financial Control for Non-Financial Managers, David Irwin, Pitman, 1995

Planning to Succeed in Business, David Irwin, Pitman, 1995

Section 8

Financial Control for Non-Financial Managers, David Irwin, Pitman, 1995

Planning to Succeed in Business, David Irwin, Pitman, 1995

Business Accounting, Frank Wood, Pitman, 1993

Accounts Demystified, A Rice, Pitman, 1993

Section 9

Financial Control, David Irwin, Pitman, 1991

Managers Guide to Financial Control, David Irwin, Pitman, 1995

Planning to Succeed in Business, David Irwin, Pitman, 1995

Business Accounting, Frank Wood, Pitman, 1993

Understanding Your Accounts,
A St John Price, Kogan Page,1991

Accounts Demystified, A Rice, Pitman, 1993

Section 10

Key Management Ratios, Ciaren Walsh,
FT/Pitman Publishing, 1993

Financial Control, David Irwin, Pitman, 1991

Section 11

*Financial Control for Non-Financial
Managers*, David Irwin, Pitman, 1995

Investment Appraisal, G Mott,
M&E Handbooks, 1993

Section 12

*Financial Control for Non-Financial
Managers*, David Irwin, Pitman (1995)

Investment Appraisal, G Mott,
M&E Handbooks (1993)

Section 13

*Financial Control for Non-Financial
Managers*, David Irwin, Pitman, 1995

Section 14

Sources of Grants and Aid for Business,
ed Anthony Harrison, Gee Publishing

Government Funding for UK Business
(eighth edition), Kogan Page, 1993

*How to Apply for Grants, Loans and Other
Sources*, Harris Rosenberg,
Gee Publishing, 1995

Section 15

Factoring, How and Practice,
Freddy R Salinger, Sweet and Maxwell, 1991

Export for the Small Business,
Henry Deschampsneufs, Kogan Page, 1990

Croner's Reference Book for Exporters,
Croner Publications

*Factoring in the UK – A Report and Guide to
the Factoring Industry*, HMSO, 1994

Sections 16 and 17

*Financial Control for Non-Financial
Managers*, David Irwin, Pitman, 1995

Small Business Survival, Roger Bennet,
Pitman, 1991

How To Maintain a Positive Cash Flow,
Gillian Clegg, Business Books Limited, 1991

Section 18

Key Management Ratios, Ciaran Walsh,
FT Pitman Publishing, 1993

Section 19

A Guide to Venture Capital and the BVCA
directory are available free from The British
Venture Capital Association, BVCA

*The Realities of Raising Business Finance –
A Practical Guide*, A C Beerel,
Management Update Ltd, 1986

Managing Growth, Maureen Bennett,
Pitman, 1991

*Criteria Used by Venture Capitalists: A Cross
Cultural Analysis*, Russel M Knight

Section 21

How to Use Your Accountant Effectively,
John Spencer,
Mercury Business Books, 1991

Small Business Finance,
J Lambden and D Targett, Pitman, 1990

24 Useful addresses

Addresses and telephone numbers for your local **Business Link, Training and Enterprise Council** (**Local Enterprise Company** in Scotland) and **Local Enterprise Agency** may be found in your telephone directory.

The **Business Link Signpost** service on (0345) 567 765 can put you in touch with your nearest Business Link office. Local **Scottish Business Shops** can be contacted on (0141) 248 6014 or (0800) 787 878 for callers from Scotland. For **Business Connect** in Wales call (0345) 969 798. **Local Enterprise Development Unit** (LEDU) in Northern Ireland can be contacted on (01232) 491 031.

The **National Federation of Enterprise Agencies** can put you in touch with your nearest agency. Ring them on 01234 354055 or on the Internet at http://www.pne.org/cobweb/nfea

Shell LiveWIRE helps young people to explore the option of starting or developing their own business. Ring them on (0191) 261 5584 or look on the Internet at http://www.shell-livewire.org

Project North East has set up an Internet site which may be of interest to anyone starting or already in business at http://www.pne.org/cobweb

If you need any help working out depreciation for your business, discuss it with your accountant or your business counsellor. **Guides to Statements of Standard Accounting Practice** may be obtained from:

Institute of Chartered Accountants of England and Wales
Chartered Accountants Hall, PO Box 433
Moorgate Place, London EC2P 2BJ

Institute of Chartered Accountants in Scotland
27 Queen Street, Edinburgh EH2 1LA

Institute of Chartered Accountants in Ireland
11 Donegal Square South, Belfast BT1 5JE

Local Investment Networking Company (LINC)
4 Snow Hill, London EC1A 2BS

British Venture Capital Association (BVCA)
Essex House, 12-13 Essex Street
London WC2R 3AA

DTI Loan Guarantee Section
Level 2, St Mary's House
c/o Moorfoot, Sheffield S1 4PQ

Prince's Youth Business Trust
18 Park Square East, London NW1 4LH

Prince's Scottish Youth Business Trust
Mercantile Chambers, 6th Floor
53 Bothwell Street, Glasgow G2 6TS

British Steel (Industry) Ltd
Bridge House, Bridge Street
Sheffield S3 8NS

The Association of British Factors
1 Northumberland Street
London WC2N 5BW

Institute of Credit Management
Easton House, Easton-on-the-Hill
Stamford, Lincolnshire PE9 3NH

Inter Company Comparison
64 Paul Street, London EC2 4NA

Venture Capital Report
Boston Road, Henly-on-Thames
Oxfordshire RG9 1DY

Chartered Association of Certified Accountants

29 Lincoln's Inn Fields, London WC2A 3EE

Chartered Institute of Management Accountants

63 Portland Place, London W1N 4AB

Index

Hawksmere – focused on helping you improve your performance

Hawksmere plc is one of the UK's foremost training organisations. We design and present more than 450 public seminars a year, in the UK and internationally, for professionals and executives in business, industry and the public sector, in addition to a comprehensive programme of specially tailored in-company courses. Every year, well over 15,000 people attend a Hawksmere programme. The companies which use our programmes and the number of courses we successfully repeat reflect our reputation for uncompromising quality.

Our policy is to continually re-examine and develop our programmes, updating and improving them. Our aim is to anticipate the shifting and often complex challenges facing everyone in business and the professions and to provide programmes of high quality, focused on producing practical results – helping you improve your performance.

Our objective for each delegate

At Hawksmere we have one major aim – that every delegate leaves each programme better equipped to put enhanced techniques and expertise to practical use. All our speakers are practitioners who are experts in their own field: as a result, the information and advice on offer at a Hawksmere programme is expert and tried and tested, practical yet up-to-the-minute.

Our programmes span all levels, from introductory skills to sophisticated techniques and the implications of complex legislation. Reflecting their different aims and objectives, they also vary in format from one day multi-speaker conferences to one and two day seminars, three day courses and week long residential workshops.

For a brochure on any particular area of interest or for more information generally, please call Hawksmere Customer Services on 0171 824 8257 or fax on 0171 730 4293.

Hawksmere In-company Training

In addition to its public seminars Hawksmere works with client companies developing and delivering a wide range of tailored training in industries as diverse as retailing, pharmaceuticals, public relations, engineering and service industries such as banking and insurance – the list is long.

We specialise in a wide range of personnel topics including Personnel and Employment Law, Competencies, Empowerment, Coaching, Appraisal, Interviewing, Communication and Motivation.

The Hawksmere In-Company team is headed by Aileen Clark, who has worked extensively in management training and development for the past twenty years, building successful courses for a wide range of businesses in both the public and private sectors. Call Aileen or her team on 0171 824 8257 for expert advice on your training needs without any obligation.

Thorogood: the publishing business of the Hawksmere Group

Thorogood publishes a wide range of books, reports, special briefings, psychometric tests and videos.

Listed below is a selection of key titles.

Masters in Management

Mastering business planning and strategy
Paul Elkin   £19.95

Mastering financial management
Stephen Brookson   £19.95

Mastering leadership
Michael Williams   £19.95

Mastering negotiations
Eric Evans   £19.95

Mastering people management
Mark Thomas   £19.95

Mastering project management
Cathy Lake   £19.95

The Essential Guides

The essential guide to buying
and selling unquoted businesses
Ian Smith   £25

The essential guide to business
planning and raising finance
Naomi Langford-Wood & Brian Salter   £25

The essential business guide to the Internet
Naomi Langford-Wood & Brian Salter £19.95

Other titles

The John Adair handbook of management
and leadership – *edited by Neil Thomas*
                                                  £19.95

The handbook of management fads
Steve Morris   £8.95

The inside track to successful management
Dr Gerald Kushel   £16.95

The pension trustee's handbook (2nd edition)
Robin Ellison   £25

Reports and Special Briefings

Dynamic budgetary control
David Allen   £95

Evaluating and monitoring strategies
David Allen   £95

Software licence agreements
Robert Bond   £125

Negotiation tactics for software and hi-tech
agreements – *Robert Bond*   £165

Achieving business excellence, quality and
performance improvement
Colin Chapman and Dennis Hopper   £95

Employment law aspects of mergers
and acquisitions – *Michael Ryley*   £125

Techniques for successful
management buy-outs – *Ian Smith*   £125

Financial techniques for business
acquisitions and disposals – *Ian Smith*   £125

Techniques for minimising the risks of
acquisitions: commercial due diligence
Ian Smith & Kevin Jewell   £125

Mergers and acquisitions – confronting
the organisation and people issue
Mark Thomas   £125

An employer's guide to the management of
complaints of sex and race discrimination
Christopher Walter   £125

Securing business funding from
Europe and the UK – *Peter Wilding*   £125

Influencing the European Union
Peter Wilding   £125

Standard conditions of commercial contract
Peter Wilding   £139

To order any title, or to request more information,
please call Thorogood Customer Services on
0171 824 8257 or fax on 0171 730 4293.